ARCTIC OCEAN

GRØNLAND

Beaufort Sea

OSTROV
VRANGELA
Chukchi
Sea
POINT BARROW

RUSSIA
UNITED BROOKS RANGE
STATES
Yukon
OGILVIE
Arctic Circle
ST. LAWRENCE
Bering
Strait
Yukon
SELWYN MTS.
MACKENZIE MOUNTAINS

ELLEF RINGNES
ISLAND
PRINCE PATRICK
ISLAND
QUEEN ELIZABETH ISLANDS
BATHURST
ISLAND
BANKS
ISLAND
Melville Sound
MELVILLE ISLAND
PRINCE OF
WALES
ISLAND
SOMERSET
ISLAND
DEVON ISLAND

AXEL
HEIBERG
ISLAND
ELLESMERE
ISLAND

Baffin Bay
BAFFIN
BASIN

Gunnbjørn Fjeld 3700
Mont Forel 3360

Amundsen
Gulf
VICTORIA ISLAND
Gulf of
Boothia
MELVILLE
PENINSULA
Foxe
Basin

PENINSULA
D'UNGAVA
Ungava
Bay

BAFFIN
ISLAND
Cumberland
Sound
Davis Strait
Denmark

GREEN
ICELAND
RISE

Mackenzie Bay
ALASKA RANGE
Mount McKinley
6194
COAST MTS.
Mount Logan
5959
Mackenzie
Great
Bear Lake
Great
Slave Lake
Back
Lake Athabasca
SOUTHAMPTON
ISLAND
HUDSON
STRAIT
KAP FARVEL

BERING
SEA
NUNIVAK ISLAND
PRIBILOF
ISLANDS
ALASKA PENINSULA
KODIAK
ISLAND
Gulf of Alaska
Mount
Waddington
3994
Peace
Athabasca
CANADA
Nelson
Lake Winnipeg
Hudson Bay
BELCHER
ISLANDS
James
Bay
MONTS
OTISH
LABRADOR
BASIN
3809
Labrador
Sea

ALEUTIAN
BASIN
ALEUTIAN ISLANDS
LEUTIAN TRENCH
Gilbert
Seamount
1435
QUEEN
CHARLOTTE
ISLANDS
VANCOUVER
ISLAND
3826
NORTH
Columbia
Yellowstone
Snake
Albany
Lake Superior
Saint Lawrence
LES LAURENTIDES
Gulf of
Saint
Lawrence
NEWFOUNDLAND
CAPE BRETON
ISLAND
CAPE RACE

NEWFOUNDLAND
BASIN

AZORE
PLATEAU

Cobb
Seamount
5257
AMERICA
Great
Salt
Lake
GREAT
BASIN
SIERRA
NEVADA
CASCADE RANGE
COAST RANGES
ROCKY MOUNTAINS
GREAT
PLAINS
Missouri
Platte
CHICAGO
Lake
Michigan
Lake
Huron
Lake Erie
Lake
Ontario
Montreal
CAPE COD
NEW YORK
MID-ATLANTIC RIDGE
AÇORES
AZORES
ATLANTIC

MENDOCINO FRACTURE ZONE
UNITED STATES
Pikes Peak 4301
OZARK
PLATEAU
Ohio
APPALACHIAN MOUNTAINS
6309

PACIFIC
5120
Mount Whitney
4418
Colorado
86
Arkansas
Red
Mississippi
NORTH AMERICAN
BERMUDA
BERMUDA ISLANDS
RISE
Sea
4689

MURRAY FRACTURE ZONE
LOS ANGELES
MEXICO
Brazos
Rio Grande
Houston
BLAKE PLATEAU
BASIN
Sargasso
6995

BAJA
CALIFORNIA
BAJA
CALIFORNIA
SEAMOUNT
PROVINCE
Tropic of Cancer
Gulf of
Mexico
MEXICO
BASIN
Straits of Florida
BAHAMA
ISLANDS
WEST
INDIES
OCEAN
1429

CABO
SAN LUCAS
SIERRA MADRE ORIENTAL
Pico de Orizaba
5610
YUCATAN
PENINSULA
Canal de
Yucatán
CUBA
GREATER ANTILLES
8605
CLARION
FRACTURE ZONE
ISLAS
REVILLAGIGEDO
SIERRA MADRE
DEL SUR
CIUDAD DE MÉXICO
MEXICO CITY
MIDDLE
CAYMAN
TRENCH
JAMAICA
HISPANIOLA
PUERTO
RICO
LESSER ANTILLES
CAPE VERDE
BASIN
7292

5720
AMERICA TRENCH
6662
Caribbean Sea
4347
VENEZUELAN
BASIN

CLIPPERTON
FRACTURE ZONE
ÎLE CLIPPERTON
4086
ISTMO DE
PANAMA
Trinidad
VENEZUELA
GUIANA
BASIN

ISLA DEL
COCO
COCOS RIDGE
ISLA DE
MALPELO
COLOMBIA
LLANOS
Orinoco
ARCHIPIÉLAGO DE COLÓN
GALAPAGOS ISLANDS
5349
Equator
6310
Chimborazo
Negro
Amazon
Belém
Equator

5485
ÎLES MARQUISES
PUNTA PARIÑAS
SELVAS
Madeira
Tapajós
Xingu
Tocantins
São Francisco
SOUTH
BRAZIL
PONTA DO SEIXAS
Recife
61

ÎLES
TUAMOTU
4389
Nevado
Huascarán
6746
LIMA
PERU TRENCH
AMERICA
BOLIVIA
BRAZIL
BASIN

ÎLES AUSTRALES
PACIFIC
4525
329
Lago
Titicaca
ILHAS M.

SEAMOUNTS
Tropic of Capricorn
EAST
PACIFIC
CHILE TRENCH
8064
GRAN CHACO
PARAGUAY
SÃO PAULO
CABO FRIO
RIO DE JANEIRO
5754

ISLA SALA Y GÓMEZ
ISLA DE PASCUA
EASTER ISLAND
ISLA SAN FÉLIX
ISLA SAN
AMBROSIO
Nevado Ojos
del Salado
6893
Paraná
ARGENTINA
URUGUAY
Uruguay
Rio de la Plata
BROMLEY
PLATEAU

OCEAN
RISE
3841
Cerro Aconcagua
6959
SANTIAGO
ARCHIPIÉLAGO
JUAN FERNÁNDEZ
PAMPA
42
Lagoa dos Patos
BUENOS AIRES
5266
ARGENTINE
BASIN

SOUTHWEST
Golfo San Matias

PACIFIC
4755
3350
SOUTHEAST
CHILE RISE
PATAGONIA
TIERRA
Cerro
San Clemente
4058
Golfo San Jorge
CABO TRES
PUNTAS
6212
FALKLAND
ISLANDS

BASIN
4876
Estrecho
de Magallanes
RIO GRANDE
FALKLAND PLATEAU
SOUTH GEORGIA

Map from Goode's World Atlas
1993 by Rand McNally, R.L. 93-S-175

Enchantment of the World

THE UNITED STATES OF AMERICA

By R. Conrad Stein

Consultant for the United States of America: Theodore Karamanski, Ph.D., Professor of History, Loyola University, Chicago, Illinois

Consultant for Reading: Robert L. Hillerich, Ph.D., Professor Emeritus, Bowling Green State University, Bowling Green, Ohio; Consultant, Pinellas County Schools, Florida

CHILDRENS PRESS®
CHICAGO

Fort Sumter,
where the
Civil War began

Project Editor: Mary Reidy
Design: Margrit Fiddle

Library of Congress Cataloging-in-Publication Data

Stein, R. Conrad.
    The United States of America / by R. Conrad Stein.
        p.   cm. – (Enchantment of the world)
    Includes index.
    Summary: Discusses the geography, history, government,
people, and culture of the U.S.A.
    ISBN 0-516-02623-2
    1. United States–Juvenile literature. [1. United States.]
I. Title. II. Series.
E156.S74   1994   93-35492
973–dc20   CIP
                                                                    AC

Picture Acknowledgments
AP/Wide World Photos: 41 (center), 53, 54, 59 (left), 61, (2 photos),
89 (top & bottom left), 93 (center & right), 94 (bottom left & bottom
right), 93 (3 photos), 99 (6 photos), 105 (left)
The Bettmann Archive: 22 (right), 24 (top & bottom left), 27 (left),
30, 35 (inset), 37 (right), 39 (left), 46 (left), 47, 48 (right), 50 (top &
bottom right), 84 (2 photos), 92 (right), 97 (bottom right), 101 (left,
top & bottom right), 103 (top & bottom left), 104 (left)
Cameramann International, Ltd.: 5, 26 (left), 66 (right) 70, 76, 113
(top left), 122 (right), 127 (bottom right), 130 (right)
Dembinsky Photo Associates: ⁹ **F. J. Baker,** 21; ⁹ **Willard Clay,** 79;
⁹ **Stan Osolinski,** 128
⁹ **John Elk III:** 24 (right), 71 (right), 117 (top right), 120 (top right),
121, 125 (right), 129 (right), 134, 137 (right)
⁹ **Virginia R. Grimes:** 125 (center)
H. Armstrong Roberts: 27 (right), 31 (inset), 38 (left), 39 (right), 41
(left), 46 (right), 50 (left), 51 (left), 97 (bottom center & left, top
center & right), 110 (left); ⁹ **George Hunter,** 10; ⁹ **Geopress,** 10;
⁹ **Camerique,** 74; ⁹ **Kord,** 114 (bottom); ⁹ **J. Nettis,** 77; ⁹ **P. Burd,** 79
(inset); ⁹ **R. Krubner,** 113 (bottom), 123 (top); ⁹ **J. Blank,** 116 (left),
131 (bottom); ⁹ **E. Cooper,** 137 (left); ⁹ **T. Dietrich,** 142 (right)
⁹ **Larry Hamill:** 20
⁹ **Jerry Hennen:** 120 (bottom)
⁹ **Emilie Lepthien:** 57, 126 (right)
⁹ **Norma Morrison:** 72 (right), 73 (right)

**National Portrait Gallery, Smithsonian Institution, Washington,
D.C.:** 41 (right)
North Wind Picture Archives: 26 (right), 31, 38 (right), 48 (left), 51
(right), 97 (top left)
Odyssey/Frerck/Chicago: ⁹ **Robert Frerck,** 67 (right), 69 (inset), 74
(bottom inset), 82, 106, 108 (top left), 129 (left); ⁹ **Walter Frerck,** 78,
81
PhotoEdit: ⁹ **Robert Brenner,** 8; ⁹ **David Young-Wolff,** 15; ⁹ **Rhoda
Sidney,** 145
Photri: 35, 37 (left), 43 (left & right), 45, 53 (inset), 72 (left), 101
(center), 102 (right), 103 (right), 117 (top center), 127 (bottom), 139;
⁹ **Bill Barley,** 4, 118 (right); ⁹ **Ramon Scavelli,** 94 (center); ⁹ **Robert
J. Bennett,** 116 (top right); ⁹ **Mike Pattisall,** 116 (bottom right);
⁹ **Roloc,** 135 (right)
R/C Photo Agency: ⁹ **Richard L. Capps,** 122 (left)
Root Resources: ⁹ **Wanda Christl,** 67 (left); ⁹ **Garry D. McMichael,**
71 (left); ⁹ **Ken Laffal,** 110 (right); ⁹ **Mary A. Root,** 114 (top), 119
(bottom left); ⁹ **Paul C. Hodge,** 117 (top left); ⁹ **James Blank,** 124
(top right); ⁹ **Richard Jacobs,** 124 (bottom); ⁹ **Russel A. Kriete,** 142
(left); ⁹ **Kohout Productions,** 143 (left)
⁹ **James P. Rowan:** 14 (left)
⁹ **Bob & Ira Spring,** 17, 128 (inset)
Tom Stack & Associates: ⁹ **Larry Lipsky,** 14 (right); ⁹ **Steve
Elmore,** 109; ⁹ **Brian Parker,** 119 (top left); ⁹ **David L. Brown,** 127
(top); ⁹ **Stewart M. Green,** 130 (left); ⁹ **Greg Vaughn,** 138 (right)
Stock Montage: 92 (left); ⁹ **1991 HPS, Inc.,** 32
⁹ **Lynn M. Stone:** 68
Tony Stone Images: ⁹ **Lawrence Migdale,** Cover (top left);
⁹ **Anthony Blake,** Cover (top right); ⁹ **Brian Seed,** Cover (bottom
left); ⁹ **Robert Frerck,** Cover (bottom right); ⁹ **Doris De Witt,** 25;
⁹ **Henley and Savage,** 88 (right); ⁹ **William S. Helsel,** 108 (top
right); ⁹ **Lois Moulton,** 108 (bottom left), 138 (left); ⁹ **Lorraine
Rorke,** 113 (top right); ⁹ **Ed Simpson,** 115; ⁹ **Don Smetzer,** 118
(left), 132; ⁹ **Leonard Lee Rue III,** 119 (top right); ⁹ **John Elk,** 119
(bottom right); ⁹ **Don & Pat Valenti,** 123 (bottom left); ⁹ **William
Means,** 123 (bottom right); ⁹ **Mark Segal,** 125 (right); ⁹ **Raymond
Barnes,** 127 (center); ⁹ **David Madison,** 135 (left); ⁹ **Joseph
Nettis,** 136 (left); ⁹ **Glen Allison,** 136 (right); ⁹ **Cliff Hollenbeck,**
141
SuperStock International, Inc.: 29, 33, 54 (inset), 86 (3 photos), 94
(top left); ⁹ **Karl Kummels,** 6, 111, 112, 126 (left); ⁹ **Steve Vidler,** 11,
18; ⁹ **Joseph D. Barnell,** 22 (left); ⁹ **C. Ray Moore,** 59 (right);
⁹ **Shostal,** 62 (left), 117 (bottom left); ⁹ **H. Eisenberg,** 66 (left);
⁹ **Robert Llewellyn,** 69; ⁹ **Herb Levart,** 89 (right); ⁹ **Gary Neil
Corbett,** 120, (top left); ⁹ **Gregory Martin,** 133 (2 photos); ⁹ **Craig
Varden,** 144
⁹ **Steve Terrill:** 140
Travel Stock: ⁹ **Buddy Mays,** 143 (right)
UPI/Bettmann: 62 (right), 73 (left), 94 (top right), 102 (center & left),
104 (right), 105 (right)
Valan: ⁹ **Stephen J. Krasemann,** 74 (top inset); ⁹ **Kennon Cooke,**
108 (bottom right); ⁹ **Hälle Flygare,** 131 (top)
Len W. Meents: Maps on 107, 109, 111, 117, 123, 131, 133, 138, 142,
143
Courtesy Flag Research Center, Winchester, Massachusetts 01890:
Flag on back cover
Cover: Some ethnic American foods include Asian (top left),
African-American (top right), Mexican (bottom left), and German
(bottom right)

Every year children compete in an Easter egg rolling contest on the White House lawn.

TABLE OF CONTENTS

Chapter 1

YEARNING TO
BREATHE FREE

She rises majestically over Liberty Island in New York Harbor. On a clear day her torch can be seen from the deck of a ship many miles out at sea. Her complete name is *Liberty Enlightening the World.* But most people call her the Statue of Liberty. For more than one hundred years she has been the nation's shining light—a symbol of hope that greets new citizens as they arrive on America's shores.

The United States is a nation of immigrants. Except for the American Indians and Eskimos, all other citizens are descendants of those who came within the last four centuries. A long history of immigration has given the United States one of the most diverse populations on earth. Its people reflect just about every race and national origin that can be found in the world.

The people who came to the United States, which was part of the "New World," sought a better life. The vast majority of them achieved their goal. The United States is blessed with fertile soil and ample water. Natural resources such as coal, iron ore, and oil abound. A wealth of other natural resources coupled with the energy of its people has given the United States a productive economy. No other nation produces so many goods and services. Americans enjoy a high standard of living.

Opposite page: Liberty Enlightening the World *on Liberty Island in New York Harbor*

The United States has an ethnic diversity.

But a powerful economy is only one element of the American story. Over the centuries Americans have added to the enrichment of world civilization. The electric lightbulb, the telephone, the phonograph, and the transistor were all devised by American inventors. The country's ethnic diversity can be experienced by listening to the musical styles of jazz, Broadway musicals, and country; eating foods such as barbecue, gyros, pizza, shish kebabs, and egg rolls; visiting mosques, churches, temples, and synagogues.

Working together, the nation of immigrants has won the admiration of the world. And the immigrants continue to arrive, seeking a better life. A line of poetry inscribed on the base of the Statue of Liberty reflects the feeling of hope that radiates from America: "Give me your tired, your poor, your huddled masses yearning to breathe free."

Chapter 2

THE LAND AND PEOPLE OF THE UNITED STATES

GEOGRAPHY

The American nation is composed of fifty political divisions called states. Forty-eight of the states are contiguous, meaning their borders touch other states. Alaska and Hawaii are separate from the contiguous states. In Alaska people refer to the contiguous states as "the lower forty-eight," while Hawaiians call them "the mainland." In terms of size, Alaska is the largest of the American states, followed by Texas and California. Rhode Island is the smallest state. The contiguous states lie in the heart of the North American continent. Their neighbors are Mexico to the south and Canada to the north.

In total area the United States covers 3,618,770 square miles (9,372,614 square kilometers), making it the fourth-largest nation in the world. Only Russia, Canada, and China have larger land areas.

Mt. McKinley in Denali National Park, Alaska

Three oceans and the waters of the Gulf of Mexico wash the shores of the United States. The Arctic Ocean forms a 1,000-mile (1,609-kilometer) coastline along Alaska's northern shore. The Pacific Ocean borders the West Coast of the contiguous states, while the Atlantic lies on the eastern shore. The Gulf of Mexico makes up a 1,600-mile (2,575-kilometer) shoreline on the southern edge of the contiguous states. Hawaii is situated in the Pacific Ocean.

LAND FEATURES

Every imaginable landscape–from deserts to rain forests and from arctic mountains to tropical shores–is found in the United States. In Death Valley, California, the land sinks to a low point of 282 feet (86 meters) below sea level. The nation's highest point is Mt. McKinley, also called Denali, in Alaska, which soars 20,320 feet (6,194 meters) above sea level.

Many kinds of vessels use the Mississippi River at New Orleans.

Three major land features stand out on a topographical map of the contiguous states: To the east the Appalachian Mountains rise, in the west the Rocky Mountains and other ranges reach the Pacific Coast, and in between the two mountainous regions are the broad central plains. Winding through the middle of the plains is the Mississippi River. The Mississippi is the largest river in North America. Its name is derived from an Indian word meaning, "father of all the waters." To the north are the Great Lakes, the world's largest freshwater reserve. Five lakes make up the Great Lakes system, but only one–Michigan–lies wholly within the United States. The other Great Lakes are shared with Canada.

The United States enjoys a fantastically diverse landscape. Majestic forests cover wilderness areas in the northern half of the country. The richest forests are found in the Pacific Northwest–northern California, Oregon, and Washington–where Douglas firs

Death Valley in the California desert

and Ponderosa pines tower to the height of a ten-story office building. The desert land east of the Rocky Mountains possesses its own haunting beauty. Great natural wonders such as the Grand Canyon in Arizona thrill visitors from around the world.

The landscape creates a wildly varying climate. The temperature extremes recorded around the country attest to the weather's great range. The temperature once dropped to 80 degrees below zero Fahrenheit (minus 62.3 degrees Celsius) at Prospect Creek, Alaska, and it climbed to a broiling 134 degrees Fahrenheit (56.7 degrees Celsius) at Death Valley, California. Annual rainfall varies from a scant 2 inches (5 centimeters) on the California desert near Death Valley to 460 inches (1,168 centimeters) on the slopes of Mt. Waialeale in Hawaii.

Generally the southern contiguous states have warmer winters than the northern ones. For example, the average January

The weather can bring beautiful snow and disastrous hurricanes.

temperature in the southern state of Georgia is 50 degrees Fahrenheit (10 degrees Celsius), while the state of Illinois in the north has an average January temperature of 30 degrees Fahrenheit (minus 1 degree Celsius). Weather in the United States can be harsh and even deadly. Cities in the Northeast and Midwest are often blanketed by blizzards in the winter. Hurricanes strike the southern states along the Atlantic coast and the Gulf of Mexico coast. Hurricane Andrew, which swept through southern Florida in 1992, killed 52 people and left a quarter million people homeless.

POPULATION AND POPULATION CENTERS

In terms of population, the United States is the world's fourth-largest nation, trailing China, India, and Russia.

The state of New Jersey has the highest population density of any state, and Alaska is the least densely populated. Holding more than 23 million people, California is far and away the most populous state. New York is the second most-populous and Texas is third.

Today three of every four Americans live in cities or towns. During the nation's first census, taken in 1790, only one person in fifteen resided in towns, and the rest of the people were rural dwellers. The census of 1920 marked the first time that more than half the American people lived in cities. By 1980 the country had more than 160 cities with a population greater than 100,000. America's most populous cities are New York, Los Angeles, Chicago, Houston, and Philadelphia.

European settlement of the contiguous states began mostly on the East Coast and pushed steadily westward. The march west can be seen in the movement of the population center, an imaginary dot placed at the mathematical middle of the American population. In 1800 the population center lay in the state of Maryland, just a few miles from the Atlantic shore. By 1980 the center of population had shifted to Missouri, crossing the Mississippi River for the first time in history.

The Spanish colonists and explorers moved into Florida and then west, crossing the Mississippi River and spreading to the West Coast. They set up missions and other settlements and then moved northward.

WHO ARE THE AMERICANS?

The poet Walt Whitman once described the complex makeup of the American people with these lines:

These states are the amplest poem
Here is not merely a nation but
a teeming Nation of nations.

Whitman's poem, written more than one hundred years ago, remains true today. African-Americans make up 12 percent of the population, Hispanics 7 percent, Asians 1.5 percent, and American Indians 0.5 percent. White Americans can trace their origins to every country in Europe. The American nation is truly an ethnic crazy quilt. Over the centuries people from every corner of the world have added to the richness of the United States.

The first large group of colonists came, mostly from Great Britain, in the 1600s and the 1700s. Also during that time masses of Africans arrived. The Africans, who were taken from their lands and transported to the United States as slaves, were the only ethnic group that came against their will. A second wave of newcomers from Europe, numbering about 7.5 million people, arrived between 1820 and 1870. Included in this second wave were thousands of Irish who came to escape famine.

On the West Coast Chinese immigrants began to come during the 1850s. An estimated ten thousand Chinese laborers helped build the western leg of the first transcontinental railroad, which began operation in 1869. In the late 1880s Japanese immigrants also reached America's shores.

Between 1880 and 1920 the third and largest group of newcomers arrived at New York harbor, where most of them passed through the huge immigrant receiving station at Ellis Island. Some 24 million people, mostly from southern and eastern Europe, came, fleeing poverty and overcrowding in their homelands.

A fourth great immigration movement began in 1965 when laws were changed to permit more people from Asian and Latin American countries to enter the United States. Some 200,000 people from war-torn Vietnam had settled in the United States by 1980.

THE GOVERNMENT

Government buildings abound in Washington, D.C., the nation's capital. Prominent among the structures are the White House, the Capitol, and the Supreme Court building. In these three government offices decisions affecting the lives of all Americans are made. The buildings house the most important government bodies created by the United States constitution. A remarkable document, the constitution was written in Philadelphia in 1787.

The Capitol is where Congress meets.

The constitution divides the federal government into three departments: the executive, the legislative, and the judicial. The executive department is headed by the president, who commands the armed forces and wields great power over foreign affairs. The legislative department is made up of two bodies–the Senate and the House of Representatives–together called the Congress. The legislative department creates new laws and rescinds old laws. The judicial department is headed by the Supreme Court, the nation's highest judicial body.

Dividing the functions of government into three departments is called the "separation of powers," or the "system of checks and balances." In theory, each department serves as a watchdog over the others.

The Supreme Court Building

The process of creating a new law illustrates how the separation of powers works. A proposed new law (called a bill) is debated by members of the House of Representatives and the Senate. When a majority of both bodies approves a bill, it goes to the president. Once signed by the president, the bill becomes the law of the land. The president may refuse to sign (veto) the bill, but the legislative department can override a veto if two-thirds of the Congress votes against the veto. After the bill becomes a law, there is always a chance it will be reviewed by the judicial department. The Supreme Court may declare a law void if members of the court believe it violates the constitution.

Chapter 3

THE BEGINNINGS

THE FIRST AMERICANS

The human race was more than two million years old before men and women entered the American continent. Those first Americans were nomadic hunters who had lived in Asia. Archaeologists theorize that they followed herds of animals across a land bridge that once existed in the Bering Sea and connected Asia and present-day Alaska. It is believed the people pushed onto the North American continent some forty thousand years ago.

In about 2000 B.C. the hunters living in the Americas developed agriculture. Corn was one of their earliest crops. Farming allowed the people to live in permanent villages and gave them spare time to fashion tools and decorate pottery. Shards of pottery are found in many sites where ancient Americans lived.

In the Ohio River valley farming groups began to construct curious earthen mounds. Initially the mounds were simple

The Great Serpent Mound in Ohio

structures designed as resting places for honored dead. The first mounds rose around 1000 B.C. As the centuries passed, the mounds became more complex. Near Hillsboro, Ohio, stand the remains of the Great Serpent Mound, which from the air looks like a giant snake. The largest mounds were built in the Mississippi River region between A.D. 700 and A.D. 1500. An incredible mound complex, called Cahokia, rose in what is now southern Illinois. Cahokia was a holy city that held as many as forty thousand inhabitants. For unknown reasons mound building ceased in the late 1500s.

Another great civilization developed in the Southwest, where farming people built houses of carved stone and adobe brick. Some of the structures were giant "apartment houses" that served as living quarters for scores of families. But the culture that constructed the buildings mysteriously faded away, and their cities lay in ruins when Spanish explorers rode through the region.

The ancient Anasazi ruins attract many tourists.

Local Navajo people told the Spaniards the cities were built by an amazing people that they called the *Anasazi*–the old ones.

THE VISITORS

Storytelling was a passion among the Viking people who lived in Iceland northeast of North America. According to one of their stories, the Viking sea captain Leif Eriksson led a flotilla of ships into unknown waters to the west of Iceland during the year 1002. After many stormy weeks Eriksson and his crew climbed ashore on a new land where they discovered a patch of wild grapes they could use to make wine. Eriksson called the country *Vinland*, "Wineland."

For generations, historians believed the Viking stories to be merely interesting works of fiction. But little by little evidence of Viking presence in the New World emerged. In the 1960s

Christopher Columbus (left) and John Cabot (right)

archaeologists digging in the Canadian province of Newfoundland uncovered the ruins of a Viking settlement that could have been Eriksson's Vinland. Today it is generally believed the Vikings were the first Europeans to have stepped upon American soil.

The visionary Christopher Columbus finally turned Europe's attention to the New World. Columbus believed he could reach the spice-rich lands of Asia by heading west from Europe and sailing around the world. Sponsored by King Ferdinand and Queen Isabella of Spain, Columbus set forth in 1492 across the broad Atlantic. He overcame furious winds and near mutiny among his terrified crew. After almost three months at sea the exhausted sailors touched land at San Salvador in the Caribbean Sea. Columbus believed he had arrived in the Indies Islands, and called the native people Indians.

A host of explorers followed Columbus. In 1497 John Cabot, an Italian navigator commanding an English ship, probed the North

American shores off present-day Canada. About ten years later Cabot's son, Stephen, sailed along the North American coast near what is now Virginia and North Carolina. Columbus himself made three more voyages to the New World, and died believing the rich Indies Islands lay somewhere near the Caribbean Sea.

THE SPANISH AND THE FRENCH

Spanish adventurers were the first Europeans to colonize the New World. The Spaniards were daring, ambitious men who relished battle and believed it was their holy duty to spread the Christian religion. Above all, the Spaniards sought gold. Historians have summed up their mission in the New World with three words: God, gold, and glory.

From the Caribbean islands the Spanish *conquistadores*, "conquerors," stormed through Cuba and landed on the shores of Mexico. The people of Mexico fought the invaders valiantly, but the Spaniards possessed two magical weapons. First they carried the powerful "thunder sticks" that could kill an opposing soldier from a distance. Most fearsome of all, however, was the conquistador cavalry. Never before had American Indians seen a horse. At first the Mexican Indians believed the horse and rider were one and the same being.

With the Caribbean and Mexico in their fold, the Spaniards looked north for new conquests. In 1540 Francisco Vazquez de Coronado led an army into the southwestern United States, venturing as far northeast as present-day Kansas. A later group of Spaniards settled in New Mexico, where they founded the city of Santa Fé in 1610. Florida, too, was a prize of the conquistadores. In 1565 the Spaniards established St. Augustine on the eastern coast

French explorers Jacques Cartier (top left) and Samuel de Champlain (left) explored Canada and the St. Lawrence River. Spaniards founded St. Augustine, the oldest European settlement (above).

of Florida. Today St. Augustine is recognized as the oldest European settlement in the United States.

Far to the north French explorers probed the shores of present-day Canada. Jacques Cartier sailed up the St. Lawrence River in 1535, and Samuel de Champlain made an even deeper penetration of the St. Lawrence in the early 1600s. Following charts drawn by Champlain, French missionaries traveled up the St. Lawrence and built a fort on an island in the river in 1642. The settlement at the fort grew to become the city of Montreal.

The dense forests of Canada teemed with fur-bearing animals. In Europe a hat made from beaver skin or a coat sewn of fox pelts was literally worth its weight in gold. Seeking fresh harvests of furs, French traders sailed boldly into the Great Lakes region. Occasionally the traders fought with the Indians, but more often a mutually beneficial partnership was formed. Many traders married Indian women. The famous fur trader Robert Cavelier, Sieur de La

The reconstructed James Fort at Jamestown

Salle, journeyed through the Great Lakes, crossed inland to the Mississippi, and followed that river south to the Gulf of Mexico.

THE ENGLISH

English colonists were latecomers in the New World. England's first serious attempt at settlement took place in 1585 at Roanoke Island off the coast of North Carolina. The Roanoke colony had a baffling fate. Three years after the people came ashore, a supply ship discovered crude buildings still standing, but not a single English man, woman, or child could be found. Historians have since called the Roanoke settlement the "Lost Colony."

In 1607 three ships anchored in the mouth of Chesapeake Bay, and a small band of frightened, half-starved English colonists climbed ashore in Virginia. The colonists built a fort there and called their settlement Jamestown, after the English king. Jamestown was the first permanent English colony in America.

A statue of Pocahontas (left) stands in Jamestown. An illustration shows Squanto greeting the Pilgrims (above).

Other English colonists, most of them seeking religious freedom, followed. The Pilgrims, who had separated from the Church of England, founded Plymouth Colony in Massachusetts in 1620. Between 1628 and 1630 the Puritans also established religious settlements in Massachusetts. English Roman Catholics, led by Leonard Calvert, built colonies on the Maryland shore in 1632.

The people of the fledgling English colonies endured hunger, disease, exposure to the cruel winter, and occasionally the threat of Indian attacks. Though they regarded Indians as enemies, they were often helped by their Indian neighbors. In Plymouth Colony an Indian named Squanto taught the colonists how to plant corn. Particularly generous was the Indian princess Pocahontas, who gave food to the starving men and women of Jamestown. According to John Smith, the leader of the Jamestown settlement, Pocahontas was, "next under God [as] the instrument to preserve this colony from death, famine, and other confusion."

African slaves being brought ashore in Jamestown (left)
and slaves working on a tobacco plantation (right)

The Indians had never been exposed to some of the "Old World" diseases carried by the colonists and they had no immunity. Between 1500 and 1600, when the Indians had initial contact with the Europeans, many Indians died from diseases such as smallpox. In some places as much as 90 percent of the Indian population was wiped out. This unintended disaster was one of the greatest tragedies in American history.

Tobacco, a native American crop, rescued the southern colonies from desperate poverty. Pipe smoking became popular in England despite the objections of the king, who called tobacco a "scurvy weed." The cultivation of tobacco brought the first large-scale use of slaves to the English colonies. By the 1660s tobacco plantations thrived in the colonies of Maryland and Virginia. Many plantations employed twenty or more slaves.

COLONIAL AMERICA

England emerged as the dominant colonial power in the present-day United States by the mid-1700s, as thirteen English colonies, holding some 1.3 million settlers, stretched along the Atlantic from New Hampshire south to Georgia. At that time, about 200,000 slaves lived in the colonies, mostly in the South. Other colonial powers, such as the French, the Spanish, and the Dutch, had comparatively small settlements in North America.

Most English colonists were hard-working, frugal people who undertook the long, dangerous Atlantic voyage because of the promises America offered. Land in the colonies was cheap and the soil was fertile. The possibility existed for a free man to arrive on American shores penniless and become a prosperous farmer within a few years. No other place on earth offered an Englishman such rapid opportunities for advancement.

From the beginning of settlement, the people established a form of democracy in the English colonies. Sheriffs and other township officers were elected. The New England colonies called town meetings to discuss community projects such as road building and bridge construction. Yet large classes of people were excluded from this democratic process. Voting was limited to free adult males who owned property. Women, slaves, and the very poor had no vote.

Colonial life was a mixture of trials and triumphs. The greatest danger the farming communities faced was rampaging epidemics of diseases such as smallpox and yellow fever that swept the settlements. Doctors were rare in colonial America, and sick people were nursed with teas made from roots and herbs that were thought to be medicinal. In villages, weddings were gigantic feasts that sometimes lasted two or three days. For recreation, colonial men raced horses, while groups of women chatted and stitched blankets in "quilting bees." Most colonists were deeply

Patriots in Boston burned stamps to protest the Stamp Act.

religious, and sometimes overzealous in their devotion. Religious fanaticism gripped the town of Salem, Massachusetts, in 1692. Terrified townspeople, believing the devil himself had descended upon Salem, hanged nineteen residents as witches.

A NATION IS BORN

There was little friction between the colonies and the mother country of England until the French and Indian War, from 1756 to 1763. It was a conflict between France and Great Britain that was often fought on American shores. Great Britain won the war, but the war effort drained its treasury. To help pay for the British troops stationed in America, the British Parliament passed the Stamp Act. Stamps had to be purchased for legal documents, such as mortgages and licenses. Newspapers also needed stamps. The Stamp Act was the first internal tax England had ever levied on the colonies, and it sparked riots. Tax collectors were beaten and

An illustration showing the Boston Massacre of March 5, 1770

driven out of town by enraged colonists. The colonists had no representatives in Parliament, and they raised the cry, "Taxation without representation is tyranny." Finally Parliament rescinded the Stamp Act, but the seeds of rebellion were planted in the colonies.

As tension between the colonies and the mother country grew, England sent an army to occupy New York City and Boston. On March 5, 1770, crowds in Boston jeered the British soldiers. The soldiers panicked and fired into the crowd, killing five people. One of the victims of the "Boston Massacre" was a runaway slave, Crispus Attucks, who today is hailed as the first African-American hero.

The bitter feelings between England and the colonies erupted into warfare on April 19, 1775. At a bridge near Concord, Massachusetts, a raging group of colonists challenged a British regiment. Rifle fire exploded, and men from both sides fell dead

A painting of the Battle of Concord (above) and Thomas Jefferson (right)

or wounded. The battle later inspired the poet Ralph Waldo Emerson to write these lines:

> Here once the embattled farmer stood
> And fired the shot heard round the world.

On July 4, 1776, a hastily organized revolutionary government issued the famous Declaration of Independence. The declaration was a brilliantly worded document written mostly by the Virginian Thomas Jefferson. It declared that "all men are created equal," and they are entitled to "life, liberty, and the pursuit of happiness." In a truly earth-shaking sentence, the Declaration of Independence forged the concept of American democracy by stating: "Governments are instituted among men, deriving their just powers from the consent of the governed." This meant that Americans would accept no form of government other than one that had been approved by the people. This was not a new idea, but acting on the idea was breathtaking in its boldness.

George Washington confers with French General Lafayette at Valley Forge.

The Declaration of Independence was also a declaration of war. The conflict pitted the loosely organized colonies against what was then the mightiest power on earth. At first it seemed as if the rebellion would collapse under British might. The British navy controlled the seas. British soldiers occupied New York and Philadelphia. In December 1777, George Washington led an ill-equipped army of eleven thousand to winter quarters at Valley Forge, Pennsylvania. Many of Washington's men had no rifles, and at least half lacked shoes.

General Washington was free to leave Valley Forge and find more comfortable quarters elsewhere, but he chose to remain with his men. In the blowing snow and howling winds, many of the soldiers became ill. At least three thousand of the men died and hundreds more deserted. Those who remained, however, formed a tough and determined army willing to follow General Washington

A portrait of Benjamin Franklin

in the battles to come. The awful winter at Valley Forge transformed Washington's men into a formidable force.

Miraculous news came from overseas, where the seventy-one-year-old Philadelphian, Benjamin Franklin, promoted the American cause in Paris, France. A writer, an inventor, and a businessman, Franklin was also a shrewd diplomat. He appealed to French government leaders to join the rebellious Americans and strike a blow at England, the ancient enemy of France. Franklin was a powerful salesman, and early in 1778 France declared war on England. After France's move Spain and Holland joined the conflict against the English monarch.

Overpowered by the Americans and their European allies, the British were forced into peace negotiations. The crushing blow came with the American-French victory at Yorktown, Virginia, in October 1781. To the world's amazement, the one-time colonists had vanquished the powerful British Empire.

Chapter 4

THE TRIALS OF
A NEW NATION

THE BIRTH OF THE CONSTITUTION

The end of the Revolutionary War left the infant United States a country with thirteen separate governments. Acting under a system of laws called the Articles of Confederation, each former colony ruled as if it were a sovereign nation and paid little regard to the central government. The lack of a strong national government gave rise to problems. For example, the war left the nation badly in debt, but it was unable to repay its creditors because the nation had no power to tax.

Hoping to design a new structure of government, delegates from every state except Rhode Island met in Independence Hall in Philadelphia during the summer of 1787. The meeting is now called the Constitutional Convention. Guiding the delegates was James Madison, a scholarly lawyer from Virginia. Madison, who later became the nation's fourth president, told the gathering of fifty-five representatives that the document they were about to write "would decide forever the state of republican government."

Above: Delegates sign the Constitution.
James Madison (inset)

With Madison orchestrating the debates, the hard work of
writing the rules for a new government began. Step by step the
document spelled out the powers to be assumed by the federal
government and those to be reserved to the states. A compromise
between the small states and large states was worked out by
creating a congress with two bodies–the House of Representatives,
whose membership would be determined by population, and the
Senate, where each state would have two members. The outcome
of the convention was the constitution of the United States. For
more than two hundred years the constitution has been the
framework of American government.

Ten important amendments were attached to the constitution
shortly after it was written. The first ten amendments guaranteed
Americans certain personal liberties, such as freedom of speech,
freedom to choose religion, freedom of the press, and the freedom

to assemble. Called the Bill of Rights, the ten amendments were added to the constitution at the urging of Thomas Jefferson.

Though the constitution was without question an ingenious document, it all but ignored the question of slavery. George Mason, from the slave state of Virginia, refused to sign the finished constitution because it left the institution of slavery undisturbed. But the majority of delegates decided to simply overlook the slavery issue. No one asked the slaves their opinion. Certainly the Fifth Amendment, which held that no person should be "deprived of life, liberty, or property," rang hollow to the nation's 700,000 African-American slaves.

THE MARCH WESTWARD

Years before George Washington was elected the nation's first president, a remarkable American named Daniel Boone discovered an Indian path leading through a gap in the Appalachian Mountains to the untouched land of Kentucky. Boone marveled at Kentucky's fresh meadows and vast herds of deer and buffalo. He helped establish a farming community in Kentucky while he continued to explore the wilderness farther west. When Boone was asked why he was forever combing the forests for new land, he answered, "Elbow room. I need more elbow room."

Boone echoed the feelings of other restless pioneers who lived in America's log-cabin frontier. A yearning to push west seemed to be innate in some Americans. At first the nation saw "the west" as the forested lands beyond the Appalachian Mountains. Soon the westward movement carried Americans over the Mississippi and to the shores of the Pacific Ocean.

Congress encouraged the development of the western frontier

*Above: An artist's depiction of Lewis and Clark with their
interpreter Sacajawea   Right: Daniel Boone*

with the passage of the Northwest Ordinance in 1787. The
Northwest Ordinance laid down rules as to how territories in the
Midwest could become states. Most important, the ordinance
guaranteed that the new states coming into existence would be
equal in every way to established states.

In 1803 President Thomas Jefferson negotiated the Louisiana
Purchase with France. For $15 million the United States bought
almost 900,000 square miles (2,331,000 square kilometers) of land,
stretching from the Mississippi River to the Rocky Mountains.
Called "the biggest real estate deal in history," the Louisiana
Purchase almost doubled the size of the United States. To explore
the new land, Jefferson sent William Clark and Meriwether Lewis
on a mission of discovery that took the explorers to the Pacific
coast. The men commanded by Lewis and Clark canoed, climbed,
and hiked over more than 3,000 miles (4,828 kilometers) of
wilderness territory.

Left: Settlers raced into Oklahoma Territory to claim land in 1889. Right: Much of the Southwest was ceded to the United States after the Mexican War.

By the 1840s the nation's march westward had gained an almost religious zeal. Many Americans believed it was God's will for their culture to spread from the Atlantic to the Pacific. The doctrine of American westward expansion was called *manifest destiny*. The spirit of manifest destiny can be seen in a speech given in the 1840s by a New Jersey political leader: "Make way for the young American buffalo—he has not land enough. . . . I tell you we will give him Oregon for his summer shade and the region of Texas as his winter pasture. . . . The mighty Pacific and the turbulent Atlantic shall be his."

Blocking the country's march westward were the northern territories of Mexico, which embraced most of the southwestern states and California. In 1835 American settlers living in Texas broke away from Mexico and formed a separate republic. The Texas question and other boundary disputes led to the Mexican War, which began in 1846. As a result of the war the United States acquired Mexico's northern lands. Also in 1846 Great Britain dropped its claims on what are now Washington and Oregon. With the acquisition of the new territory, manifest destiny

Gold was discovered at John Sutter's mill (left) and thousands of people came to pan for gold (right).

was complete. America now stretched "from sea to shining sea."

California paid immediate rewards to the nation. In 1848 a worker digging at John Sutter's ranch in present-day Sacramento uncovered a few specks of gold. The discovery triggered the great California Gold Rush, a wild mass movement of people. Some eighty-five thousand gold seekers swarmed to California in 1849 alone.

But looming over the nation during its advance to the Pacific was the daunting question of slavery. President Jefferson once warned his countrymen that the slavery issue hung over them, ringing "like a fire bell in the night."

A HOUSE DIVIDED

Tice Davids ran for his life. It was the spring of 1831 and Davids, a slave, had escaped from his Kentucky plantation. After running through the woods for days he reached the Ohio River. But his master and a team of dogs were just minutes behind. Davids plunged into the icy waters of the Ohio and swam toward a riverbank village. Then his luck suddenly changed. Davids climbed out of the river at the slavery-hating town of Ripley, Ohio. To his surprise the escaped slave saw a white man frantically beckoning him into his house. His rescuer was John Rankin of the "Underground Railroad." Davids had discovered the path to freedom.

The Underground Railroad was a loosely organized group of men and women who helped slaves flee to communities in the northern states or to Canada. In their work they used railroad terms. The person guiding the slaves was called the "conductor," and the houses providing temporary hiding places were referred to as "stations." The most celebrated conductor on the Underground Railroad was Harriet Tubman, herself an escaped slave. In her career Tubman guided more than three hundred runaways to freedom. Each time she ventured into the south she faced re-enslavement or the death penalty.

By the 1850s the Underground Railroad was just one of many abolitionist groups that had developed in the country. The abolitionists sought to abolish slavery. The fiery speaker Frederick Douglass was one of the most famous American abolitionists. Douglass, who escaped from a slave master at age twenty-one, told a cheering crowd at an antislavery meeting, "I appear this evening as a thief and a robber. I stole this head, these limbs, this body from my master, and ran off with them."

As the abolitionist movement grew, the nation divided into separate, dangerously hostile camps. Fistfights broke out in Congress, and a shooting war raged in Kansas between pro-slavery and antislavery forces. The extension of slavery into the new states developing in the west became a burning issue.

Into this explosive environment stepped Abraham Lincoln, the

Left to right: Abraham Lincoln, Frederick Douglass, and Harriet Tubman

tall politician from Springfield, Illinois. A product of the log-cabin frontier, Lincoln was largely self-educated. Yet he became a successful lawyer. His folksy backwoods manners allowed him to win over a jury of farmers, and his deep intelligence permitted him to sway a highly educated judge. Lincoln ran for president in 1860 when the slavery issue had already torn the nation apart. He opposed slavery, but he was no firebrand abolitionist. "As I would not be a slave, so I would not be a master," he once said. Lincoln hoped slavery would simply die a natural death. He was, however, opposed to extending slavery into the western states.

When Lincoln won the presidential election of 1860, the southern states refused to accept him as their leader. By the time Lincoln took his oath of office, seven southern states had already seceded from the union to form their own government, called the Confederacy. On April 12, 1861, Confederate artillery fired on

Federal troops at Fort Sumter in Charleston, South Carolina. The cannon fire plunged the country into a brutal civil war.

Lincoln and millions of his countrymen had seen the conflict approaching like a dark cloud on the horizon. Two years before his election Lincoln had warned his fellow Americans, "A house divided against itself cannot stand. I believe this government cannot endure, permanently, half slave and half free."

BROTHER AGAINST BROTHER

The Civil War, fought from 1861 to 1865, was one of the bloodiest conflicts in American history. Until the Korean and Vietnam Wars, the Civil War held the dubious distinction of being the war in which the most Americans were killed. The Civil War left the nation with deep emotional scars that took generations to heal.

Clearly, the Union forces, led by Lincoln, had superior resources when the war began. The states of the North had more than twenty-two million people, compared to nine million in the South. And the South's population included four million slaves who could not be called on to fight and who posed a constant threat of rebellion. Northern states had double the railroad mileage of the South and triple the number of factories. New York State alone had more factories than the entire Confederacy. But despite their disadvantages, the southern states scored stunning victories early in the war. The Confederate army was blessed with brilliant generals such as Virginia's Robert E. Lee. The Union, on the other hand, had military leaders who were plodding and indecisive.

During the war neither side enjoyed political unity. Northern states such as Indiana, Ohio, and Lincoln's own Illinois contained

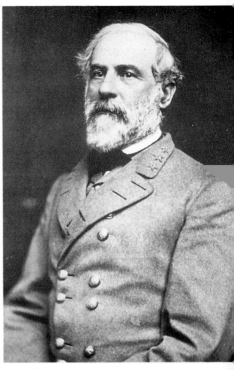

At the Battle of Gettysburg (above), illustrated by Currier and Ives, the Confederate army headed by General Robert E. Lee (right) was forced to retreat.

thousands of southern sympathizers. Cities in the northeastern states teemed with immigrants who had no interest in fighting America's wars. When President Lincoln ordered a military draft, the Irish immigrants in New York City rioted and two thousand people were killed. The South, too, held masses of people who were pro-Union. Only one of four southern white families owned slaves, and many southerners were opposed to the institution of slavery. Virginians had such divided loyalties that farmers in the western part of the state broke away to form West Virginia.

The turning point of the Civil War came in July 1863, at the tiny town of Gettysburg, Pennsylvania. General Lee hoped to take the offensive by marching his armies north, but he was met at Gettysburg by northern forces numbering eighty-five thousand men. For three days the two armies engaged in battle. Lee was forced to retreat after suffering twenty thousand casualties. After Gettysburg, the Confederate army was never able to regain its strength.

On New Year's Day in 1863, President Lincoln issued the

Emancipation Proclamation, which freed all slaves in those southern states occupied by Union troops. At that time Lincoln also decided to recruit African-American soldiers into the Union army. By late 1864 one of every ten Union troops was African-American, and African-American regiments had fought in many major battles. Twenty-three African-American Civil War soldiers won the Congressional Medal of Honor for courage under fire.

After four years of bloody fighting, the end of the war came on April 9, 1865, when Robert E. Lee surrendered to Union General Ulysses S. Grant at Appomattox, Virginia. On April 14 Abraham Lincoln attended Ford's Theater in Washington, D.C. There John Wilkes Booth, a southern sympathizer, sneaked into the president's box and shot him in the head. Lincoln died on April 15, 1865. The assassination, coming so close to the end of the war, moved Walt Whitman to write a famous poem ending with the lines:

> Exult O shores, and ring O bells!
> But I with mournful tread,
> Walk the deck my Captain lies,
> Fallen cold and dead.

RECONSTRUCTION AND RECOVERY

The war left the South in ruins. Reporter John Trowbridge toured Richmond, Virginia, the capital city of the old Confederacy, and saw "cellars half filled with bricks and rubbish . . . impassable streets deluged with debris [and] iron fragments of crushed machinery." Yet the economic base of the South—its fertile land—could not be destroyed. Just a year after the last shot was fired, the cotton fields and tobacco plantations bloomed again. Political recovery proved to be a slower and more painful development.

After the Civil War much of the South, including Richmond (left), Virginia, was in ruins.

Lincoln had hoped to bring the southern states back into the Union "with malice toward none, with charity toward all." But the post-Civil War Congress, led by a group called the Radical Republicans, wanted to punish the eleven southern states for the sin of secession and ensure civil rights for the newly freed slaves. Opposing the Radicals was President Andrew Johnson, who had served as vice-president under Lincoln. The president and Congress clashed over the program called Reconstruction, which was designed to restore the American Union and expand its democracy. Early in the Reconstruction years Congress held sway, and the South was occupied by military forces.

Caught in the middle of the bickering were the freed slaves. At first the African-Americans benefited from Reconstruction. The Thirteenth Amendment to the constitution ended slavery, and the Fourteenth Amendment gave African-Americans the right to vote and to hold political office. For several years after the war African-Americans held seats in state legislatures and in the United States Congress. However, southern whites soon reestablished political power and took the teeth out of Reconstruction laws.

Segregation for African-Americans in the South extended to separate drinking fountains (left). The Ku Klux Klan (right), a white supremacist group

Some southern whites turned to violent organizations to suppress the African-Americans. In the Reconstruction years the secret society called the Ku Klux Klan (KKK) rose to power in the South. Klan members wore white sheets or robes to portray themselves as the avenging ghosts of slain Confederate soldiers. In the southern states KKK members stormed through their communities to hang, whip, and tar-and-feather troublesome African-Americans or their white supporters.

By the late 1870s Reconstruction had ended, and so had African-American aspirations for full citizenship in the South. Devious twists in state laws denied southern African-Americans the vote. Throughout the South the "color line" was drawn. African-Americans were required to wait for a train at a separate part of the platform, and to ride in "colored only" cars. Schools were segregated, as were restaurants, hotels, and theaters. Segregation extended to public bathrooms and even water fountains. Almost a century would pass before another revolutionary would erase the color line.

Chapter 5

A WORLD POWER

Railroad officials and workers celebrated when the Union Pacific and Central Pacific trains met at Promontory, Utah, on May 10, 1869.

INDUSTRY, PROGRESS, AND CHANGE

At a dusty plain in Utah well-dressed dignitaries stood alongside laborers clad in overalls. A brass band played patriotic music. On a single railroad track two engines, facing each other, inched closer. It was May 10, 1869, and the dignitaries were about to drive in a gold spike marking the completion of the first transcontinental railroad. The engineering feat required the labor of twenty thousand men who hammered down 1,100 miles (1,770 kilometers) of track in just under three years. The golden spike ceremony moved author Bret Harte to write:

> What was it the engines said,
> Pilots touching, head to head,
> Facing on the single track,
> Half a world behind each back?

The expansion of the railroads is just one phase of the Industrial Revolution that engulfed the United States in the late

Early skyscrapers (left) used elevators developed by Elisha Otis and electric lightbulbs invented by Thomas Edison (above).

1800s and early 1900s. Factories sprouted up, churning out newly developed products such as phonographs, typewriters, and the gasoline-powered automobile. Mechanical reapers and other farm implements relieved farmers of many backbreaking tasks and made American farms more productive. Between 1870 and 1915 the value of goods coming from American factories and farms increased tenfold.

The Industrial Revolution brought dramatic changes to the cities. Electrically powered streetcars replaced the horse-drawn trolleys that had carried passengers for generations. In the late 1800s skyscrapers began looming over the horizons of Chicago, New York, and Philadelphia. The towering buildings were served by elevators developed by Elisha Otis. The offices in the buildings were illuminated by small electric lightbulbs invented by Thomas Edison, who worked in a laboratory in New Jersey.

The riches reaped by industrial expansion bred fantastic fortunes. Andrew Carnegie of Pittsburgh, Pennsylvania, built a giant steel corporation and became one of the world's richest men. John D. Rockefeller of New York established the Standard Oil Company and controlled the country's petroleum industry. Marshall Field of Chicago grew rich by operating a highly successful department store.

During these confident years, while business expanded wildly, the United States made its last territorial acquisitions. In 1867 Secretary of State William Seward purchased Alaska from Russia for $7,200,000–a real estate deal that cost about 2 cents an acre. Despite the bargain price, many Americans criticized the purchase, calling it "Seward's Folly." The United States took possession of the Hawaiian Islands in 1898 and in the same year fought the brief Spanish-American War. Because of the war the nation acquired Guam, the Philippines, and Puerto Rico. The Philippines were granted independence in 1946. Guam and Puerto Rico remain United States territories. In Puerto Rico the people are periodically asked to vote on whether they wish to keep their present status or become an American state.

In 1903 the United States purchased a narrow strip of land across the Isthmus of Panama and constructed the engineering masterpiece called the Panama Canal. The Panama Canal Zone remains an American territory, but a treaty allows Panama to take control of the Zone and the canal on December 31, 1999.

The American conservation movement took its first giant step in the beginning of the twentieth century. President Theodore Roosevelt, who was president from 1901 to 1909, was an avid hiker, mountain climber, and wilderness lover. During Roosevelt's administration 150 million acres (60,703,500 hectares) of land were

Above: President Theodore Roosevelt served from 1901 to 1909. At that time thousands of immigrants were being processed through Ellis Island every day. Top right: Processed immigrants wait for a ferry to take them to New York City. Right: Italian immigrants wait to be processed.

added to the national forest system and five new national parks were created. The first national bird reservations and game preserves were set up under Theodore Roosevelt's leadership.

THE WORLD OF THE IMMIGRANT

Supplying the muscle for the nation's industrial expansion were recent immigrants from Europe. Between 1870 and 1916 more than twenty-five million people, mostly from southern and eastern Europe, landed on American shores. For most, their long sea voyage ended at Ellis Island, a rocky outcropping in New York Harbor. The federal government built an immigration processing center on Ellis Island in 1892, and soon afterward some ten thousand newcomers passed through its Registry Hall each day. Today it is estimated that one of every four Americans has an ancestor who was processed through Ellis Island long ago.

Many Asian immigrants arrived on the West Coast, such as these Japanese (left) who landed at Seattle. Ethnic stores were opened by immigrants. This Chinese grocery store (right) in San Francisco provided familiar products.

On the West Coast Asian immigrants faced great hostilities from the white majority. In 1882 alone more than forty thousand Chinese took up residence in the United States, most of them settling in California. The Chinese were hard working, law-abiding people. But whites, especially in California, felt they were being overwhelmed. Responding to pressure from West Coast citizens, Congress passed a law banning Chinese immigration. In the early 1900s masses of Japanese began arriving on the West Coast, and they were greeted by new laws that prohibited them from owning property and forced their children to go to segregated schools.

Immigration slowed when Europe exploded into World War I in 1914. Three years later the United States, now a global power, entered the war. The war ended in 1918, and soon afterward Congress passed a law restricting immigration from southern and eastern European countries. Because of the law, the flood of immigrants was reduced to a trickle.

BOOM AND BUST

The 1920s were called the "Roaring Twenties." It was a decade
when youth rebelled and adults broke the law every time they
drank a glass of beer. In 1919 the Eighteenth Amendment to the
constitution had been approved. The amendment prohibited the
sale or manufacture of alcoholic beverages in the United States.
But the attempt to better the lives of Americans by banning
alcohol proved to be a failure. No law in American history was
more openly violated than Prohibition. In city neighborhoods
illegal bars called "speakeasies" opened for business. Criminal
gangs supplied beer and spirits to a thirsty America. Chicago's Al
Capone owned a beer and liquor empire worth millions of dollars.

Heroes of the Roaring Twenties loomed as larger-than-life
figures. The decade's most celebrated hero was a congressman's
handsome son from Minnesota, Charles Lindbergh. On May 20,
1927, Lindbergh climbed into a tiny single-engine aircraft and took
off from a muddy field in New York State. In the air he pointed
his plane toward the Atlantic Ocean. Twenty-two hours later
Lindbergh landed in Paris, becoming the first aviator to fly the
Atlantic alone. Upon his return Lindbergh was given one of the
most joyous parades in New York City's history.

During the 1920s even waitresses and office boys bought shares
of companies on the New York Stock Exchange. In this decade of
prosperity, an investment in stocks could double in just a year.
But in the fall of 1929 prices on the New York Stock Exchange
began to waver. On October 29—Black Thursday—stock market
prices collapsed. A typical disaster was the price of stock in the
White Sewing Machine Company, which dropped from $48 a

As a few wealthy people arrive at Times Square to attend a Broadway theater during the Depression, a long line of unemployed (above) wait to receive a meal. Charles Lindbergh (inset) became a hero after his solo flight across the Atlantic Ocean.

share to less than $1 a share in an afternoon. It is estimated that Black Thursday cost investors $40 billion.

The stock market crash was the start of the Great Depression that gripped the nation and the world in the 1930s. Banks failed, crop prices plummeted, and businesses closed. By 1932 one in four Americans had lost their jobs. The prosperous people of the 1920s now found themselves sewing patches on old clothes and stuffing cardboard into their shoes to cover the holes. A young girl who once lived in a comfortable Cleveland home remembered, "My father lost his job and we moved into a double garage. . . . It was awful cold when you opened those garage doors. We would sleep with rugs over the top of us. Dress under them."

Despairing Americans turned to a new leader–Franklin Delano Roosevelt–to bring them out of the Depression. Roosevelt was born into a wealthy New York family and grew up in a thirty-

WPA workers (above) were used to build sidewalks and pave roads. President Franklin Roosevelt's frequent talks on the radio (right) were called "fireside chats."

room mansion. At age thirty-nine Roosevelt was stricken with polio and lost the use of his legs. (Until a vaccine was discovered, the disease of poliomyelitis caused crippling and other muscle disorders.) Refusing to allow his disability to slow him down, Roosevelt won a landslide victory for the presidency in 1932. Although the nation's economy was mired in the Depression, Roosevelt's inaugural address sounded as positive as a trumpet salute: "First of all, let me assert my firm belief that the only thing we have to fear is fear itself."

Roosevelt launched a whirlwind program designed to provide Depression relief. A government agency called the Works Progress Administration (WPA) gave jobs to unemployed men and women. Many WPA projects involved paving rural roads and building sidewalks in the cities. But the WPA also gave useful work to writers and artists. WPA artists painted twenty-five hundred murals on the walls of public buildings, and agency writers wrote an outstanding guidebook for each of the forty-eight states.

The Social Security Act of 1935 established pensions for retired persons and insurance for the unemployed. Other people, including the disabled, benefited from this act. Roosevelt called his program of government activism the New Deal. While Roosevelt could not end the Depression, the New Deal gave Americans faith in the power of government and hope for the future.

WAR AND THE POST-WAR PERIOD

World War II began in Europe in 1939 when Nazi Germany, led by Adolf Hitler, marched into Poland. Britain and France declared war on Germany. In 1940 Germany advanced on other European countries and countries in North Africa. Many countries were overcome and occupied by Germany and their allies, the Italians. The Japanese, who were also allied with Germany, began conquering nations in the Far East.

Sunday, December 7, 1941, was a sunny and warm day at the United States naval base at Pearl Harbor, Hawaii. Hundreds of soldiers and sailors walked to church that morning. They heard the buzzing of distant airplanes, but paid little attention to the sound. Then, suddenly, Japanese aircraft swarmed over the base, raining bombs on the airfields and on the battleships tied up at dock. A navy radio operator sent out a message that astonished the world: AIR RAID, PEARL HARBOR. THIS IS NO DRILL.

The Japanese attack plunged America into World War II. Four days after Pearl Harbor, Germany declared war on the United States. More than any other single event, the war shaped the country's destiny in the twentieth century. Some 12.5 million American men and women served in World War II, and more than 1.2 million were killed or wounded.

During the war years the nation's factories produced 300,000 airplanes, 90,000 tanks, and 11,900 ships. This amazing production record was achieved through the help of two million women who joined the work force for the first time. Before the war women were generally considered to be unfit for heavy factory work, such as building armaments. But a popular figure who emerged during the war years was "Rosie the Riveter," representing all the heroic women workers on the aircraft assembly lines.

In 1942 the Roosevelt administration launched the Manhattan Project, which produced the first atomic bomb. The Manhattan Project was so secret that even Vice-President Harry S Truman was unaware of its existence. When Roosevelt died in April 1945, Truman became president and decided to use the new weapon. Atomic bombs were dropped at Hiroshima and Nagasaki, Japan, in August 1945. The bomb's capacity for destruction shocked even its inventors. More than 92,000 people were killed in the initial blast at Hiroshima alone. The atomic bomb helped to end World War II, but it ushered humanity into the frightening Nuclear Age.

During the postwar period there was spectacular growth of American suburbs. Houses in the suburbs offered "breathing room" for working-class families from the cities. Characteristic of the new suburbs was their residents' total dependence on the automobile for transportation. Two-car and even three-car families became common in suburbia.

Soon after World War II the Cold War began. The Cold War was a tense ideological struggle between democratic nations and Communist countries, particularly the Union of Soviet Socialist Republics (USSR), that lasted more than forty years.

In 1950 soldiers of Communist North Korea invaded South Korea. President Truman sent American troops, and the fighting

A display of rockets, called "Rocket Garden," at the Kennedy Space Center in Florida

escalated when Communist China ordered its soldiers to assist the North Koreans. The Korean War dragged on for three years, cost more than fifty-four thousand American lives, and ended in a frustrating stalemate.

SPACE EXPLORATION

In the late 1950s during the Cold War the Soviet Union sent the first artificial satellite, *Sputnik I*, into orbit around the world. Then the Soviets launched their first manned space flight. The United States was not far behind. In 1962 the United States sent John Glenn into orbit and the space race was on. The first man to step on the moon was Neil A. Armstrong. Armstrong piloted a lunar module, *Eagle*, onto the moon on July 20, 1969 as Americans watched on television. Both Russia, once the largest part of the former Soviet Union, and the United States continue space exploration.

The United States space program is conducted by the National Aeronautics and Space Administration (NASA), which has headquarters at the Lyndon B. Johnson Space Center in Houston,

Texas. Space shuttles take off from the John F. Kennedy Space Center in Cape Canaveral, Florida.

Since the pioneer days of the Space Age, scientists have been able to explore the planets, the moon, and the stars. Satellites have been put into orbit to monitor weather, to transmit communication signals, and to help new scientific advancements.

THE CIVIL RIGHTS REVOLUTION

On a chilly afternoon, December 1, 1955, Rosa Parks boarded a bus in Montgomery, Alabama. Parks, a forty-two-year-old African-American seamstress, had no idea she was about to make history. She paid her dime for the fare and took a seat in the rear of the bus. Soon the bus became crowded and the driver ordered her to surrender her seat to a white passenger. In Montgomery African-Americans were not only required to sit in the back of the bus, they also were supposed to give up their seats so that no white would have to stand. But this afternoon Rosa Parks simply said no; she was too weary.

Parks was arrested, and it seemed her small act of rebellion would be quickly forgotten. But that night the members of Montgomery's African-American community met and announced they would refuse to ride the buses until the segregation policies were ended. Their hastily organized boycott was almost 100 percent effective.

Today historians point to the Montgomery bus boycott as the beginning of the Civil Rights Revolution. Since Reconstruction, brutal segregation had been the law of the land in the South. Restaurants had blaring WHITE ONLY signs in their front windows. Because they could not vote, southern African-Americans had no

Rosa Parks (left) is fingerprinted by the deputy sheriff of Montgomery, Alabama. The Reverend Dr. Martin Luther King, Jr. (right)

legal way to change the segregation laws. So the African-Americans took a more dangerous course. They broke the law by sitting in at restaurants and defiantly taking the front seats on buses. The Civil Rights Revolution of the 1950s and 1960s shook the foundation of the Old South.

A leading spokesman of the African-American crusade was the Reverend Martin Luther King, Jr., a Baptist minister. He ordered his followers to keep their protests nonviolent, even when police attacked them with their water cannons, tear gas, and guard dogs. King's greatest triumph came on August 28, 1963, when 200,000 African-Americans and whites took part in a march on Washington. There, at the Lincoln Memorial, King gave a speech that will be remembered forever: "I have a dream that one day this nation will rise up and live out the true meaning of its creed: 'We hold these truths to be self-evident; that all men are created equal.'"

Through the courts and through acts of Congress the civil rights movement achieved many of its goals. In a landmark 1954 decision the Supreme Court had held that maintaining separate school systems for African-Americans and whites was a violation of the constitution. The Civil Rights Act of 1960 put teeth in the laws guaranteeing all Americans the right to vote. The sweeping Civil Rights Act of 1964 ended segregation in restaurants, hotels, theaters, and other businesses open to the public.

Martin Luther King, Jr., remained the nation's foremost civil rights spokesman. Though he preached nonviolence, he was stabbed in New York City, stoned in Chicago, and jailed several times in the South. Then, on April 4, 1968, King was gunned down by an assassin. On his gravestone are the words of his favorite Negro spiritual: "Free at last. Free at last. Thank God Almighty, I'm free at last."

CHALLENGES AT HOME AND OVERSEAS

In 1961 John F. Kennedy was inaugurated as the nation's thirty-fifth president. He was America's first Catholic president, and at age forty-two, the youngest ever elected to the office. Kennedy was admired for his movie-star looks and for the youthful energy he brought to the White House. In office he established the Peace Corps, an organization that allowed American volunteers to work in underdeveloped lands and try to raise their standards of living. During his administration the USSR placed ballistic missiles in Cuba, and the world teetered on the brink of war until Kennedy forced the Soviets to withdraw the weapons. The nation was shocked on November 22, 1963, when President Kennedy was shot and killed by an assassin in Dallas, Texas.

Once more the torch of leadership passed, this time to Vice-President Lyndon B. Johnson. Ruling confidently over the

Left: President John F. Kennedy gives his inaugural speech.
Right: After the Kennedy assassination Lyndon Johnson, with
his wife on his right and Jacqueline Kennedy on his left,
was sworn in as president.

legislature, Johnson launched a program called the Great Society,
which was intended to eliminate poverty in America. He backed
laws giving tax funds to education and public housing. Though
he was born and grew up in Texas during the time of segregation,
Johnson supported civil rights legislation of the early 1960s.

Despite its accomplishments the Johnson administration was
stained by American involvement in the Vietnam War. The war in
Vietnam was essentially a civil war that pitted the Communist-
backed forces of the north against the United States backed
government of the south. American involvement began in the
1950s when President Dwight D. Eisenhower sent money and
weapons to South Vietnam. President Kennedy ordered military
advisers to the country. Under Lyndon Johnson American
involvement escalated to the point where a half million combat
troops fought in Vietnam in 1968. Despite the great commitment
of American forces, the war remained a stalemate. As casualties
mounted, people at home watched reports on the nightly

Showing both division and solidarity, people demonstrated against *the war in Vietnam (left) and* for *the Equal Rights Amendment (right).*

television news, and many protested American involvement in Southeast Asia. The war divided the country almost as intensely as did America's Civil War. On May 31, 1968, Lyndon Johnson made a televised speech, admitted there was "division in the American house," and announced he would not run for president again.

The 1960s and early 1970s were years of great division in America. College students, protesting the Vietnam War, took over campuses. African-Americans, frustrated by generations of poverty, rioted in the cities. The 1960s was also a period when Americans became aware of their deteriorating environment. Air and water pollution were recognized as menaces affecting the health of all citizens. Conservation groups campaigned for laws to preserve wilderness areas and to save vanishing wildlife.

The women's liberation movement, also launched in the 1960s, contained much of the passion found in the civil rights revolution. Groups such as the National Organization for Women (NOW) crusaded for equality with men, especially in the workplace. For generations women had been channeled into jobs such as secretary or file clerk, and they faced closed doors if they attempted to move up to a management position or become a professional. The women's liberation movement sponsored laws forbidding job discrimination based on sex. Buoyed by the new laws, women began to take jobs in engineering and medicine that had previously been closed to them.

Republican Richard M. Nixon was elected president in 1968. During his administration the Vietnam War finally came to an end. Nixon made a visit to China, opening relations with that country for the first time since the Korean War. Nixon was reelected to the presidency by a landslide vote in 1972. However, just before the election a group of burglars was arrested at Washington's Watergate apartment complex where the Democratic party headquarters was located. The burglars were found to be employees of Nixon's reelection committee. The president's attempt to cover up the crime enraged the American people and the Congress. Facing possible impeachment, Nixon resigned the presidency on August 9, 1974. He was the only president in history to step down from office.

During the 1970s, Presidents Gerald Ford and Jimmy Carter faced a crisis when Middle Eastern countries curtailed their shipments of oil to the United States. Gasoline shortages resulted. The gasoline crunch demonstrated the need for greater use of public transportation in the United States.

An increase in crime captured the nation's headlines in the 1980s. The decade of the 1980s was the most violent in American history, as easily acquired handguns combined with an epidemic of drug use to trigger a record number of murders. Washington, D.C., was the nation's crime center, with more murders per capita than any other city.

Overseas the dominant event of the 1980s was the collapse of communism. It began in Poland where union workers peacefully overthrew their long-standing Communist government. The anti-Communist movement then spread to East Germany and finally to the Soviet Union itself. The Soviet Union, the giant of the Communist world, became a confederation of ethnic republics, each with a capitalistic economy. The demise of Soviet communism ended the Cold War that had gripped the world for four decades.

In 1990 President George Bush sent a half million soldiers, sailors, and marines to the Persian Gulf after Iraq invaded its neighbor Kuwait. Egypt, Saudi Arabia, Great Britain, and France also moved large bodies of troops to the area. The American-led Allied force launched an air war and a brief ground war in early 1991. The Iraqi army was forced to retreat from Kuwait. But the Iraqi leader, Saddam Hussein, remained in power.

During the late 1980s and early 1990s American middle-class families sensed a downturn in their standard of living. Hospital costs soared, as did the cost of a college education for young family members. Giant corporations such as IBM and the Sears department store chain dismissed thousands of workers. Bill Clinton, the little-known governor of Arkansas, used the troubled economy as his major theme when he defeated George Bush in the presidential election of 1992.

Chapter 6

EVERYDAY LIFE

HOW AMERICANS REALLY LIVE

During the 1980s and 1990s a television program aired across the United States. "Lifestyles of the Rich and Famous" showed the mansions and the estates of leading sports figures, Hollywood stars, and top business executives. The program was a dazzling display of swimming pools, tennis courts, and customized automobiles.

Movies and television often portray the rich as typical Americans. "Lifestyles of the Rich and Famous" reinforced the notion that Americans live in luxury. However, the superrich are only a tiny fraction of America's population. The United States supports a multitude of lifestyles–from the heights of wealth to the depths of poverty. Most families fall somewhere between the two extremes.

Over the nation's history Americans have shifted gradually from a rural to an urban way of life. When the first census was taken in 1790, 95 percent of the population lived in rural areas. By 1990 about three-fourths of all Americans were urban dwellers– people who live in cities, towns, and suburbs. Since World War II, the central cities have lost population while suburban areas around them have boomed. By 1980 more people lived in suburbs than in the cities themselves.

Poverty is a problem in the United States in rural areas (above) as well as in cities (left).

In general people in metropolitan areas earn more than people in small towns and rural areas. Also, Americans who have completed college or have had professional training usually earn more than people with less schooling. In the United States, as in most countries of the world, income determines a person's material comforts in life.

In the late 1980s the United States government defined poverty as an annual income of $11,000 or less for a family of four. Nearly one-fifth of all American families fall below this poverty line. Many of America's poor people live in the inner cities. In such neighborhoods as New York City's South Bronx and Chicago's west side, youth gangs clash across a landscape of burned-out buildings. Pockets of poverty exist in rural areas as well. Many poor people struggle in the coal-mining regions of Kentucky and West Virginia, or in the farm regions of the Deep South. Life is particularly hard for migrant farm workers. Migrant workers are forced to follow the harvests of fruit and vegetables, traveling from state to state during the growing season.

A middle class neighborhood (left) and a luxury home (right)

The majority of Americans fall within the category that sociologists call the middle class. People in the middle class work at a variety of jobs: teachers, nurses, firefighters, photographers, electricians, or storekeepers. Generally, middle-class income is high enough to allow a family to own a home, buy one or more automobiles, and use laborsaving devices such as washing machines, power lawn mowers, and dishwashers. However, during the 1980s the rising costs of health care and education brought new pressures to bear on the middle class. Many people found they had to work at more than one job to pay their bills.

Despite these setbacks, the American middle class still lives comfortably. Household electricity, clean running water, and ample food are all taken for granted by the middle class. Beyond the basic necessities of life, families enjoy entertainment frills such as VCRs, stereos, and vacations within or outside the United States.

Some members of the upper class come from "old money." They live on fortunes earned by their ancestors. Others, such as sports and entertainment figures, have recently soared to millionaire status.

A junior high math class

EDUCATION

Most American children have learned about the life of Abraham Lincoln, the boy born in a log cabin who studied hard and eventually became president. Parents, teachers, and political leaders all agree that education is the key to success in the United States.

In America, individual states set standards and rules concerning education. By 1918 every state in the union had passed laws requiring school attendance, in most cases until the age of sixteen. About 80 percent of the elementary and secondary schools in the United States are public, offering education free of charge. The remainder are private schools—many of them run by religious institutions. Of the nation's high school graduates, more than half go on to higher education—college or vocational training.

America's colleges and universities are among the finest in the

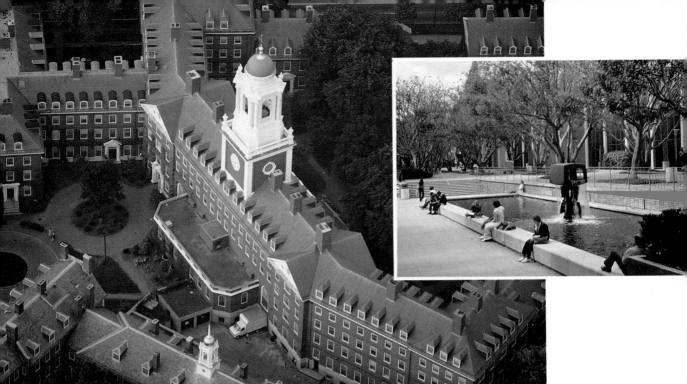

Harvard (above), founded in 1639, is one of the oldest universities. The University of California at Los Angeles (inset) is much newer–1919.

world. Many, such as the University of Wisconsin and the University of California, are vast educational systems run by state governments. Other schools are funded by religious institutions or are privately endowed. Some of the best-known institutions of higher learning are Harvard University in Cambridge, Massachusetts; Yale University in New Haven, Connecticut; Princeton University in Princeton, New Jersey; the University of Notre Dame in South Bend, Indiana; the University of Chicago in Chicago, Illinois; and the University of Texas in Austin, Texas.

The nation's extensive library system is an invaluable supplement to schools. The United States has about eight thousand public and five thousand university libraries, as well as thousands of small libraries in schools and classrooms. Public libraries are open to everyone, free of charge.

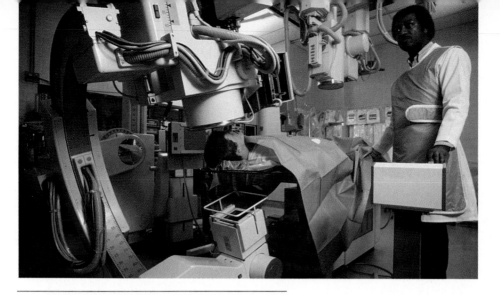

A hospital patient receives a digital angiogram test.

HEALTH CARE AND SOCIAL SERVICES

In 1990 life expectancy in the United States stood at 74.9 years. Improved sanitation and immunization against some infectious diseases greatly increased longevity during the twentieth century. Nevertheless, infant mortality remains higher in the United States than in many other industrialized nations. This demonstrates that there is still a need for better health care and health education.

American hospitals offer the benefits of modern technology, but treatment comes with a high price tag. A hospital room in an intensive-care unit had a cost of $600 a day or more in the 1990s. Although many Americans have private health insurance, the United States entered the 1990s with no nationwide program of health-care coverage. The need for a national health-insurance plan was a crucial issue in the 1992 presidential election. Former Arkansas governor Bill Clinton was elected in part because he promised to create a system of inexpensive health care for all Americans.

Health care is provided through government-funded programs such as Medicaid (for the poor) and Medicare (for people over

People are free to worship as they please. Places of worship may be old, like this mission in Texas (far left), or very modern, like St. Mary's Cathedral in San Francisco (left).

age sixty-five). Other state and federally supported programs provide financial help to people without jobs. These include Aid to Families with Dependent Children (ADC) and Supplemental Security Income (SSI). Since 1935 all working Americans have contributed to a federal Social Security fund. After retirement they receive monthly payments from this fund.

RELIGION

Many of the first colonists who came to America were fleeing from religious persecution in Europe. The United States constitution guarantees freedom of religion to all and requires a strict separation of church and state.

About 60 percent of all Americans profess a particular religious faith. Of these, 52 percent are Protestants. Protestant churches include Presbyterian, Lutheran, Episcopalian, Baptist, Methodist, and Pentecostal. Some 37 percent of Americans are Roman Catholic and 4 percent are Jewish. With increasing immigration from Asia and the Middle East, Buddhist temples and Islamic mosques have sprung up in most American cities.

The Fourth of July is celebrated with fireworks and parades.

HOLIDAYS AND CELEBRATIONS

The yearly calendar provides Americans with abundant
opportunities to reflect on the nation's history. Holidays
celebrating events and people in the American past include Martin
Luther King Day in January, President's Day in February,
Memorial Day in May, Labor Day in September, Columbus Day in
October, and Veterans Day in November. Since the 1970s these
holidays have been held on Mondays to provide workers with
long weekends. Memorial Day, which honors the dead of the
nation's wars, is usually an occasion for parades with military
bands. Independence Day, July 4, commemorating the signing of
the Declaration of Independence in 1776, is a time for thundering
fireworks displays.

The Christmas season reaches full bloom in November with
displays in store windows and a barrage of advertisements on

In December retail stores are decorated for Christmas (left). Jews celebrate Hanukkah by lighting the menorah (above).

television and radio. A religious holiday in origin, Christmas has become a key factor in American retail sales. Some businesses, such as the toy industry, say the Christmas season accounts for a major percentage of their market. But Christmas is a time of special warmth and sharing among families and friends. The ornaments that decorate the Christmas tree are a collection of memories gathered year by year. Christmas is a time for returning home, however far one has traveled.

December is also a special month for other important holidays. In the Jewish calendar it is the season for Hanukkah, the Festival of Lights. Hanukkah is an eight-day celebration of hope and faith rewarded. One of America's most recently established holidays is Kwanzaa. Drawing upon ancient African customs, Kwanzaa is an African-American celebration of renewal that coincides with the Christmas season.

Chapter 7

AMERICA AT WORK

INDUSTRIES AND THE ECONOMY

The United States is an industrial giant, dwarfing all other countries. America's Gross National Product (GNP), the combined value of all the goods and services sold each year, totals $5 trillion. Japan, which has the world's second-largest GNP, produces less than half the goods and services that the United States does. The state of California alone is such an industrial and agricultural powerhouse that if it were an independent country, its GNP would rank it among the world's top ten nations.

Despite these impressive figures, American industry faced problems near the end of the twentieth century. The country lost millions of manufacturing jobs to other nations. In the 1940s the city of Detroit, Michigan, produced half the world's automobiles; by the 1990s Detroit accounted for less than 1 percent of the world's car production.

MANUFACTURING

Manufacturing remains a dynamic industry, even though millions of jobs have been lost to overseas markets. The United

Opposite page: Natural gas, used for energy, is compressed in these tanks.
Inset above: Cowboys still exist; this one works on a ranch in Montana.
Inset bottom: A family spreads feed on their cattle and hog farm in Iowa.

A jumbo jet under construction in a giant hanger at the Boeing plant in Everett, Washington

States has 500,000 major industrial plants and many more shops and light assembly firms. About 20 million Americans–17 percent of the work force–hold manufacturing jobs. The country's five largest manufacturing companies are General Motors, Ford Motor Company, Exxon, International Business Machines (IBM), and General Electric.

Transportation equipment, including cars, trucks, buses, airplanes, and trains, is the leading enterprise. Food products–everything from canned soup to TV dinners–is the second leading category. Chemical products are third on the national manufacturing scene. California is by far the leading state in factory production, followed by New York, Ohio, Illinois, and Michigan.

For many years manufacturing was concentrated in the North, especially the Midwest. The states of Illinois, Ohio, Michigan, and

An assembly area of an electronics company

Indiana were known for their great factory complexes. But in the 1980s manufacturing shifted to the South. New factories, many of them equipped with the latest automation equipment, opened in Tennessee and North Carolina. Meanwhile, plants and equipment in the Midwest became underused and out of date. Economists began to call the once mighty Midwest the "rust belt."

MINING

Mining employs only 1 percent of the American work force, but mineral wealth has been important to the nation's growth. Coal is needed to make steel that, in turn, is used to make automobiles, bridges, and the superstructures of office buildings. States in the Appalachian Mountain region, such as Kentucky and West Virginia, are dependent on coal mining for a great percentage of their jobs.

A petrochemical complex in Houston, Texas

America's chief mineral products are—according to their dollar value—petroleum, natural gas, and coal. The United States is the world's second-largest petroleum producer, trailing only Russia. But because Americans drive cars far more than people in other nations do, the country consumes far more petroleum than it produces. Every year the United States must import millions of barrels of oil. The American petroleum industry employs 1.5 million workers and owns plants and equipment worth $330 billion. Texas, Oklahoma, Louisiana, Alaska, and California are leading petroleum-producing states.

Natural gas is often found in the same regions where underground deposits of petroleum exist. The United States is the world's second-largest natural gas producer. Natural gas is used in homes for cooking and heating, and it is used in industry to fire the furnaces and in shaping and bending metals. Gas accounts for 25 percent of the total energy used in the United States.

Feed corn (inset) and a field of soybeans

Other important minerals taken from United States soil include copper, gold, granite, iron ore, limestone, phosphate, sand and gravel, and sulfur.

AGRICULTURE

American farmers are the most productive in the world. The average American farmer produces enough food each year to feed eighty people. The country's farms regularly provide enough food for American citizens and ship their excess abroad. America accounts for 25 percent of the world's beef supply and 15 percent of the world's grain supply. No other nation sends more food to foreign markets than does the United States.

The United States has 2,300,000 farms. The average American farm is 440 acres (178 hectares). Most are family owned. Overall more than 1 billion acres (more than 400 million hectares) of

American land is devoted to farms and ranches. Only 3 percent of the total American work force is employed on farms. Despite the small number of farm workers, the United States is productive because of the fertile soil, ample rainfall, and the best laborsaving equipment used by the farmers.

California is the leading farm state, followed by Iowa, Texas, Nebraska, and Illinois. The nation's most productive single agricultural area is California's Central Valley, where a sunny climate and extensive irrigation allow farmers to harvest four crops a year. The flat and level Great Plains states, such as Iowa and Nebraska, are centers for wheat and corn growing. Wisconsin is called "America's Dairyland" because of its devotion to milk and milk products. Texas leads all other states in beef production.

TRANSPORTATION

The country has fifty-five cars for every one hundred people. In rural areas even impoverished people own automobiles (although perhaps not the latest models).

The nation's road network includes 3,900,000 miles (6,276,270 kilometers) of streets, highways, and roads. The Pennsylvania Turnpike, opened in 1940, was the first modern superhighway. A nationally financed highway program, begun in 1956 and not completed until the early 1990s, created the giant belts of superhighways that crisscross the country today. It is now possible to drive from New York City to Los Angeles and never once encounter a traffic light. Such a trip would have been considered miraculous to drivers fifty years ago.

But Americans have paid a heavy price for their dependence on automobiles for transportation. During rush hours some city

Most metropolitan areas have heavy traffic during rush hours.

streets become snarling traffic jams. The cities' six-lane
expressways fare no better. Pollution that fouls the air over urban
areas comes mainly from motor vehicle emissions. In recent years
cities and suburbs have turned more toward mass transit to get
people to and from their jobs.

Subways are the most efficient form of mass transit.
Underground trains speed people from station to station with
little pollution and no traffic tie-ups. The New York City subway
is one of the biggest and busiest in the world. Subways also
operate in San Francisco, Atlanta, Baltimore, Chicago,
Philadelphia, and Washington, D.C. Mass transit subways are
expensive to build, but no more costly than superhighways that
cut through the hearts of cities. In the 1990s even car-crazy Los
Angeles was building a subway.

Railroads carry 35 percent of the nation's freight. America has
150,000 miles (241,395 kilometers) of tracks. Before the rise of the
automobile, travelers regularly took trains from one city to

A plane landing at O'Hare International Airport in Chicago

another. Today less than 1 percent of American travelers use trains. The once elegant trains that had dining cars in which meals were served on starched white tablecloths are now a relic of the past.

About 15 percent of American travelers fly to their destinations. The United States has seventeen thousand airports, but only seven hundred are large enough to handle today's huge passenger jets. Chicago's O'Hare International Airport is the world's busiest, with fifty-six million passengers landing and taking off there each year.

Ships sailing over the Great Lakes and inland waterways carry 15 percent of the nation's freight. The huge ships and barges carry bulk loads far cheaper than do trucks or railroads. America's leading port cities that receive oceangoing ships are New Orleans, New York, and Houston.

SERVICE INDUSTRIES

A service worker is one who performs a service rather than creates a product. For example, a bagger in a supermarket checkout station is a service worker. Teachers, doctors, social workers, waitresses, and bookkeepers are service workers. The service field holds by far the bulk of the country's jobs. Almost three out of every four Americans are classified as service workers. One of the fastest growing fields in the service area is that of health care.

FOREIGN TRADE

The United States exports high technology equipment including computers, precision measuring devices, and special purpose engines. Heavy equipment like tractors and earthmoving machines also are manufactured in the United States and sold abroad. Corn, wheat, beef, soybeans, and other agricultural products are regularly exported to foreign markets.

But since the 1980s the United States has bought more goods from abroad than it has sold to foreign sources. Practically every TV and VCR sold in American stores today was manufactured elsewhere. A large percentage of the cars driven in the United States come from foreign companies. A nation that buys more goods from abroad than it sells is said to have a poor balance of trade or a trade deficit. In 1991 the United States had a record trade deficit of $99 billion. A trade deficit is damaging to the economy because it costs the nation jobs.

John Singleton Copley's painting,
Boy with a Squirrel *(right)*
and an Asher Durand landscape (below)

Chapter 8

ARTS AND
ENTERTAINMENT

The United States thrives largely because its people are hardworking. But Americans love their leisure time too. Sports, the arts, and a host of other activities occupy Americans after working hours. Literature and the fine arts have had a proud history in the nation.

THE FINE ARTS

Few masterful painters lived and worked in colonial America. John Singleton Copley, who was born in Boston in 1738, was an exception. Copley's painting, *Boy with a Squirrel,* so impressed English experts that they persuaded Copley to study in their country. Copley set up a studio in London and became a popular painter there.

America's great natural beauty inspired artists of the early 1800s to paint sweeping outdoor scenes. Painters such as Thomas Cole and Asher Durand used the magnificent Hudson River valley as a base when rendering landscape paintings and developing what is called the Hudson River School. Another painter drawn to the

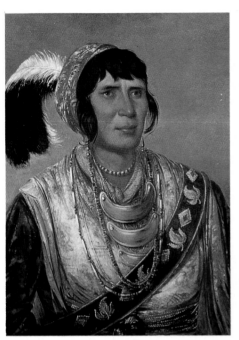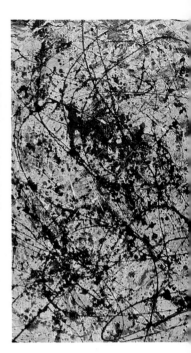

Left to Right: Osceola *by George Catlin,* The Child's Caress *by Mary Cassatt, and* Reflections of the Big Dipper *by Jackson Pollock*

outdoors was George Catlin, born in Pennsylvania in 1796. Catlin ventured into the wilderness regions of the Mississippi River to paint scenes of Indian villages and portraits of powerful chiefs.

In the late 1800s America's painters became increasingly influenced by the artistic revolution taking place in Europe. Mary Cassatt, born to a wealthy Pennsylvania family in 1844, did much of her painting in France. Cassatt painted stunning pictures, often of women and children. Pennsylvania-born Thomas Eakins also went to France to study. Eakins returned to the United States and devoted his life to teaching and portrait painting.

Stark realism presided over American painting in the early twentieth century. The challenge of the boxing ring was brutally brought to life in a 1924 George Bellows painting showing a grim-faced fighter knocking his opponent through the ropes. Thomas

Hart Benton of Missouri trekked the back roads during the 1920s and 1930s to paint scenes of farmers at work and at play. Grant Wood's painting, *American Gothic,* is a classic portrait of an Iowa farm couple. The loneliness of big city life was a favorite topic of Edward Hopper, who lived in New York City. Hopper's 1942 work, *The Nighthawks,* portrays three customers and a counterman sitting at an all-night café with the lights above them casting an eerie glow.

Post World War II American art embraced wildly varying themes. Jackson Pollock, of New York City, produced abstract paintings using revolutionary techniques such as dropping paint onto canvas. One of the most important of America's modern artists was Georgia O'Keeffe, who lived in Taos, New Mexico. Some of O'Keeffe's paintings are close-ups of animal skulls, bleached white by the desert sun. The tiny town of Taos, where O'Keeffe settled, remains an artist colony.

ARCHITECTURE

In colonial America the South led the North in erecting fine houses and buildings. Many wealthy plantation owners built mansions resembling English manor houses. Upper-class residents of Charleston, South Carolina, designed elegant three and four-story town houses that are the pride of the city today. Williamsburg, Virginia, once the capital of Virginia Colony, is also a showcase of southern colonial architecture. Williamsburg now boasts more than eighty restored buildings that date back to the 1700s. One of the South's most gifted architects was Thomas Jefferson, the nation's third president. Jefferson designed his own

Colonial Williamsburg (above) has been restored.
Monticello (right), was Thomas Jefferson's home.

home, the handsome Monticello, and he drew plans that were used for the first buildings of the University of Virginia.

The creation of Washington, D.C., in the late 1700s and early 1800s, was a major architectural achievement. Washington was a planned city, designed from the start so the Capitol building would be at its center. The architect of the nation's capital was Pierre Charles L'Enfant, a French engineer hired by George Washington. L'Enfant was assisted by American surveyors Benjamin Banneker and Andrew Ellicott. Banneker was a self-educated free African-American man who was also prominent as a mathematician and astronomer.

Chicago became the birthplace of modern architecture after a fire leveled its business district in 1871. Rising from the ashes of the Chicago Fire were new high-rise buildings supported by a lightweight steel frame instead of thick walls. The revolutionary buildings with "curtain walls" enabled architects to add more

Frank Lloyd Wright (top left) designed the Falling Water house (above). Ludwig Mies van der Rohe (bottom left) is known for the steel and glass skyscrapers he designed.

windows and present an openness that previous buildings lacked. Leading members of the Chicago School of architecture included William Le Baron Jenney, Louis Sullivan, and Daniel Burnham.

One of America's great modern architects was Frank Lloyd Wright, who was born in Wisconsin in 1867 and remained an active architect until his death in 1959. Wright's Robie House, built in Chicago in 1909, established his famous Prairie Style, a low, horizontal design graced with many porches and terraces. Other Wright masterpieces include Falling Water, a house built over a waterfall in Bear Run, Pennsylvania; the Johnson Wax Building in Racine, Wisconsin; and the Guggenheim Museum in New York City.

Glass and steel skyscrapers, designed in the International Style, dominate the skyline of American cities today. The master of the International Style was German-born Ludwig Mies van der Rohe, whose gleaming glass and steel towers rose in the 1940s and

1950s. Eventually American architects rebelled at the restrictions of the International Style and created a movement called Post-Modernism, which has no identifiable form. Leading Post-Modernist architects include Peter Eisenman, Charles Moore, and Stanley Tigerman.

COMMUNICATION

"Congress shall make no law . . . abridging the freedom of speech or of the press," says the First Amendment of the constitution. Freedom of speech is the foundation behind the vast American communication industry. The country's communication network includes newspapers, magazines, books, radio, and television.

The United States has seventeen hundred newspapers that circulate sixty million copies each day. The national edition of *The New York Times* has a daily circulation of almost two million copies.

More than twelve hundred magazines—weeklies and monthlies—are read in the United States. Magazines such as the *Bulletin of the Atomic Scientists* are intended for a limited audience. *TV Guide*, which has a weekly circulation of almost seventeen million, is the most widely sold U.S. magazine. *Life Magazine* began in 1936 and since then has published some of the most dramatic news photos. In 1942 John H. Johnson of Chicago started *Negro Digest* and Johnson's company grew to include *Ebony* and *Ebony, Junior*, along with other magazines of interest to African-American readers.

Newspapers and magazines rely on sales of advertising space for revenue, because the price paid over the counter does not cover publishing costs. Each year American companies spend $110 billion to advertise in newspapers, on TV, on billboards, and in other media. No other nation advertises so heavily as does the United States.

Book publishing is a major communication industry. Each year $11 billion worth of books are sold in the United States.

About ten thousand radio stations operate in the United States. Radio's golden age came in the 1930s and 1940s when families gathered around the radio to listen to their favorite comedians, detective stories, dance music, soap operas, and news programs. In the 1950s television doomed the popularity of traditional radio shows. Radio stations, realizing that their audiences were now listening mostly in cars, turned to a news-and-music format. Radio "talk shows," where the listeners call the station and discuss everything from politics to personal problems, enjoyed growing popularity in the 1980s and the 1990s.

TELEVISION

Television in the United States boomed in its earliest years. In 1945 there were about ten thousand sets in American homes; by 1950 that number had shot up to six million, and in 1960 about sixty million households had television sets.

The ability of television news to bring events into American homes was dramatized in the 1960s. News cameras took viewers to the front lines of the Vietnam War. The cameras also filmed protests on city streets as demonstrators demanded that the United States withdraw from Southeast Asia.

During the 1970s color television replaced black-and-white sets and audiences grew. Viewers can watch soap operas, sports, dramas, talk shows, and other programs, as well as news shows.

John Philip Sousa (right), is remembered for his marches, and Stephen Foster (far right) for his songs.

AMERICAN MUSIC

Music has deep roots in America. Indians used music and dance as indispensable elements in religious ceremonies. Some groups believed their ancient songs and dances were taught to their ancestors by the gods. The colonists brought hymns from England and sang in their church services. At the time of American independence the religious sect called the Shakers had developed many songs including the song "Simple Gifts."

Some of the most lasting music to come out of the nineteenth century were the spirituals sung by African-American slaves. Songs such as "Go Down, Moses" and "Swing Low, Sweet Chariot" were sung by slaves at work and during church meetings. The most famous American composer of the nineteenth century was Stephen Foster, who was inspired by music he heard from African-Americans. Foster wrote hundreds of songs, including the favorites "Oh! Susanna" (1848), "Camptown Races" (1850), and "Jeanie with the Light Brown Hair" (1854). Toward the end of the nineteenth century John Philip Sousa composed stirring marches: "The Washington Post March," "The Stars and Stripes

Left to right: Scott Joplin's portrait appears on the cover of his music for "The Entertainer." Louis Armstrong and Benny Goodman played jazz.

Forever," and "Semper Fidelis" are only a few of them. Military bands in dozens of nations began playing Sousa's marches. He is remembered as "The March King."

African slaves sang the blues when they were working in the fields. Blues are mournful songs in which the verse of the first line is usually repeated in the second. Then the third line gives a response. Many blues describe sadness or loneliness.

Jazz–the uniquely American form of music–probably originated around the end of the nineteenth century. One of the pioneer jazz composers was the African-American pianist Scott Joplin, who composed ragtime, lively music mainly for the piano. Joplin's "Maple Leaf Rag," written in 1899, became popular throughout the nation. Joplin composed other music, including a folk opera, *Treemonisha*, that was never performed during Joplin's life.

Ragtime music merged with the blues and from this emerged jazz. During the 1920s African-American artists such as Louis Armstrong and "Jelly Roll" Morton brought jazz popularity. In the 1930s and 1940s white musicians Woody Herman, Benny Goodman, and Glenn Miller became caught up in the jazz craze and performed big band jazz and swing music in dance halls.

Important people in American music are Miles Davis (top left), Leonard Bernstein (center), Elvis Presley (top right), Aaron Copland (bottom right), and Gerry Mulligan (bottom left).

"Cool jazz" played by trumpeter Miles Davis and saxophonist Gerry Mulligan was the rage in the 1950s and 1960s. In modern times rock blends with jazz in the music of Quincy Jones.

Mississippi-born Elvis Presley emerged in the 1950s to become the king of American rock and roll music. While singing on stage Presley shook his hips wildly–a habit that shocked some people but won him devoted fans. Presley's best-known songs are "All Shook Up," "Jailhouse Rock," and "Hound Dog."

George Gershwin is an American composer of popular songs and show tunes as well as classical compositions. Some of Gershwin's great symphonic pieces are *Rhapsody in Blue* (1924), *Piano Concerto in F* (1925), and the opera *Porgy and Bess* (1935). Aaron Copland is an American classical composer who used early American folk music as themes when composing such works as *Billy the Kid* (1938), *Rodeo* (1942), and *Appalachian Spring* (1944). Leonard Bernstein is popularly known for composing the musical

Broadway musicals have been composed by George M. Cohan (left), Richard Rodgers and Oscar Hammerstein II (center), and Frederick Loewe and Alan Jay Lerner (above right).

West Side Story, but he won fame also as a conductor and as a brilliant teacher of classical music to the general public.

American musical comedy was made famous in the music halls of New York City's Broadway. In the early 1900s George M. Cohan wrote musicals containing the popular songs "I'm a Yankee Doodle Dandy," "Give My Regards to Broadway," and "You're a Grand Old Flag." Music lovers flocked to Broadway theaters to see Richard Rodgers and Oscar Hammerstein's *Oklahoma* (1943) and *South Pacific* (1949). The composer-lyricist team of Frederick Loewe and Alan Jay Lerner entertained Broadway audiences with *Brigadoon* (1947) and *My Fair Lady* (1956). Jerry Bock and Sheldon Harnick's *Fiddler on the Roof* played from 1964 to 1972. The electric rock musical *Hair* (1967), composed by Galt MacDermott, showed rebellious American youth of the 1960s. *A Chorus Line*, a musical composed by Marvin Hamlisch, opened on Broadway in 1975. By the time of its closing in 1990, it had become the longest-running show on Broadway, with more than six thousand performances.

LITERATURE

"Dear children, I leave you in an evil world that is full of snares and temptations. God only knows what will become of you." These words, spoken in the 1740s, were part of the farewell sermon of Jonathan Edwards, who was minister of Northampton, in the Massachusetts Colony. Edwards and other clergymen dominated the literature of colonial America. Each Sunday they terrified their congregations with graphic descriptions of hell's fire.

Thomas Paine was the most influential writer of the American Revolution. His pamphlet, *Common Sense*, was an argument for separation from the mother country. During the darkest days of the Revolutionary War, Paine wrote the famous lines, "These are the times that try men's souls. The summer soldier and the sunshine patriot will, in this crisis, shrink from the service of their country. . . . Tyranny, like hell, is not easily conquered."

Writers from New York State led a flowering of American literature that bloomed in the early 1800s. New Yorker Washington Irving helped to create a new form of literature—the short story—with his tales "Rip Van Winkle" and "The Legend of Sleepy Hollow." James Fenimore Cooper, who lived in upstate New York, took his readers to the thick of the American wilderness through his novels *The Last of the Mohicans* and *The Deerslayer*. Herman Melville was born in New York City and as a youth hired out on merchant ships and whaling vessels. Melville used his experiences at sea to write the exciting book *Typee* and his classic *Moby Dick*. Edgar Allan Poe wrote poems and short

Early American writers, clockwise from top left, are Thomas Paine, James Fenimore Cooper, Washington Irving, Mark Twain, Harriet Beecher Stowe, and Edgar Allan Poe.

stories. He is considered the inventor of the detective story.

A book helped to start America marching toward the bloodiest war in its history. Harriet Beecher Stowe, born in Connecticut in 1811, was a dedicated foe of slavery. In 1852 she completed her novel *Uncle Tom's Cabin*, which described the suffering of plantation slaves. The passions generated by *Uncle Tom's Cabin* hastened the onset of the Civil War.

Mark Twain, born Samuel Clemens in Missouri, was a humorist and critic of American life. About the nation's political leaders he said, "It could probably be shown by facts and figures that there is no distinctly native criminal class except Congress." Twain wrote fast-moving travel memoirs entitled *Innocents Abroad* and *Roughing It*. He is most remembered for the creation of Huckleberry Finn and Tom Sawyer, two mischievous boys growing up along the Mississippi River.

Early in the 1900s writers launched a wave of criticism against a rapidly changing America. H.L. Mencken of Baltimore blasted American culture in his many essays. Upton Sinclair exposed unsanitary conditions in meat-packing houses in his book *The Jungle*. Willa Cather, who was raised in Nebraska, wrote novels about the life of the immigrants living in Nebraska and the Southwest. *Death Comes for the Archbishop* is considered her best work. Yoknapatawpha County, Mississippi, was the fictional spot used in the novels and short stories of William Faulkner, who was from Mississippi. Faulkner's favorite novel was *The Sound and the Fury*, which he wrote in 1929.

World War I produced a group of American writers, such as Ernest Hemingway and F. Scott Fitzgerald, who were disillusioned with America's direction. Hemingway witnessed World War I as a Red Cross volunteer and other wars as a newspaper or magazine correspondent. Some of his experiences are recalled in *A Farewell to Arms* and *For Whom the Bell Tolls*. In his powerful novel *The Grapes of Wrath*, John Steinbeck followed the Depression-era journey of the Joad family from their debt-ridden Oklahoma farm to a new life in California.

Eugene O'Neill and Arthur Miller are two of the nation's well-known playwrights. O'Neill was born in New York City, the son of a prominent actor. As a young man he rebelled against his father and ran off to sea. Many of O'Neill's characters are downtrodden sailors or dock workers who aspire to lead a better life but are never able to change their circumstances. Arthur Miller's *Death of a Salesman* is the study of the disintegration of an American family. In gripping scenes Miller's characters seek meaning in their lives, only to be left empty and bewildered by the death of their salesman father.

African-American novelists brought protest literature to new

Twentieth century authors, clockwise from top left, are Ernest Hemingway, Willa Cather, Ralph Ellison, Claude Brown, John Steinbeck, and Arthur Miller.

heights in the years after World War II. The main character in Ralph Ellison's 1952 book, *The Invisible Man,* cries out, "People refuse to see me . . . When they approach me they see only my surroundings." New Yorker Claude Brown wrote a book called *Manchild in the Promised Land,* which portrayed the impact that heroin made on African-American society in Harlem. Malcolm Little became a Black Muslim because he wanted to unite blacks. His book, *The Autobiography of Malcolm X,* is a protest book about his life in small-town Michigan and in New York City.

Many social critics consider the 1980s to be a decade of greed, dominated by big business. One of the most popular novels of the 1980s was Tom Wolfe's *Bonfires of the Vanities,* which explored the inner workings of corporate America and brought readers behind the scenes into New York City's political back rooms. Characters in *Bonfires of the Vanities* reject the notion of honor and morality, desiring only riches and power.

THE MOVIES

More than any other art form, American motion pictures have spread American culture to almost every point of the globe. Movies were invented in the United States in 1889 by Thomas Edison. The American director Edwin S. Porter created the first movie that told a story in his 1903 film, *The Great Train Robbery*. By 1907 some five thousand movie theaters were in operation in the United States, and American-made films were delighting audiences abroad.

The early movies had no sound and were presented on small screens. Still, gifted directors such as D.W. Griffith created sweeping panoramas with casts of thousands. Griffith's 1915 production, *The Birth of a Nation*, was a grand-scale Civil War epic.

The silent screen era produced a host of stars who became immortals in the American mind. Charlie Chaplin, whose best-known trademarks were a derby hat and a cane, portrayed a lovable, trouble-prone little tramp who took audiences through dozens of comic adventures. Mary Pickford played fresh, wholesome roles, and won the title "America's Sweetheart." No screen lover was more adored than Rudolf Valentino, whose most famous role was that of a handsome desert aristocrat in the 1921 movie, *The Sheik.*

The 1930s are looked on as the "Golden Age of Movies." Home television did not exist at the time, and a night at the movie theater provided a refreshing lift during the Great Depression. Hollywood was in full bloom during the 1930s. In 1939 alone Hollywood studios turned out such international classics as *Gone With the Wind, The Wizard of Oz,* and *Stagecoach.*

Great directors as well as stars captured fame in the movie

Left: D.W. Griffith supervising the production of one of his films. Center: Charlie Chaplin was called "the little tramp." Above: Mary Pickford was "America's Sweetheart." Above right: Orson Welles was both an actor and a director.

industry. In 1941 the young Orson Welles directed *Citizen Kane*, the story of a powerful newspaper tycoon. Many film historians consider *Citizen Kane* to be the greatest American movie ever made. John Huston was a Hollywood maverick who directed memorable movies over a span of forty years. One of Huston's classics was the 1944 film, *Treasure of the Sierra Madre*, the spellbinding story of a man driven insane over his lust for gold.

Modern movies compete with television, and many fans complain that moviemakers employ excessive violence and nudity to draw audiences. Most of the famous studios in Hollywood now make TV dramas instead of films intended for the theaters. Still, millions of tourists stream into Hollywood every year to catch a glimpse of a well-known actor and to dream about the time when it was "Tinseltown," America's silver-screen window to the world.

Some of the well-known films Steven Spielberg (above) directed are Jaws, E.T., *and* Jurassic Park. *Joe Louis (right) was heavyweight boxing champion in the 1930s and 1940s. Babe Ruth (far right), the home-run king*

Hollywood is still the leading film center. Steven Spielberg, who made his first hit movie, *Jaws*, in 1975, produced the dinosaur film, *Jurassic Park*, in 1993. Spielberg's imagination and special effects have produced some of the most popular films ever made.

SPORTS

Americans enjoy sports. The nation's superathletes have greater popularity—and earn much more money—than government leaders. Some American sports heroes become legends. The boxer Joe Louis, the heavyweight champion of the 1930s and 1940s, is venerated in the memory of African-Americans. Louis, who grew up in Detroit, Michigan, slugged his way to the top at a time when African-Americans suffered humiliating segregation in the northern as well as the southern states. Whenever Louis fought, African-Americans hugged their radios to catch the description of each blow.

Baseball greats Ty Cobb (top left), Henry Aaron (bottom left), and Jackie Robinson (above)

American athletes excel at individual sports such as swimming, tennis, track, and boxing. But fan interest is greatest in team sports.

Baseball is so popular it is called the national pastime. But contrary to popular belief, the game was not invented by Civil War General Abner Doubleday. Instead, baseball evolved from an English game called rounders. By the early 1900s the two major leagues had formed, and America's love affair with baseball was fully established. Stars such as Babe Ruth, Ty Cobb, and Grover Cleveland Alexander thrilled fans early in the twentieth century. After being "white only" in its early history, professional baseball was integrated in 1947, when Jackie Robinson joined the Brooklyn Dodgers. In 1974 the African-American outfielder Henry Aaron hit

Above: This painting shows the first college football game between Rutgers and Princeton in 1869. Right: James Naismith, the "Father of Basketball"

his 715th home run to break the long-standing record held by Babe Ruth. Baseball, which requires little special equipment, is played in city schoolyards and in rural sandlots. To many kids the coming of spring means renewal of the baseball season, the most glorious time of the year.

American-style football evolved from soccer. The first organized college game took place in 1869, when Rutgers defeated Princeton. Today college and professional teams enjoy dizzying popularity. Once a year it seems the whole nation comes to a halt while the Super Bowl game determines the professional championship.

High school football is a passion—particularly in small-town America. Big games between arch-rival small-town teams are major events, talked about for years.

In the 1980s and 1990s Michael Jordan (left) of the Chicago Bulls was one of the most exciting basketball players in America. Kids playing in school yards or behind garages (right) wanted to be like Mike.

Basketball was invented in 1891 by James Naismith, a physical education instructor in Springfield, Massachusetts. Naismith hoped to develop a sport his students could play between the football and baseball seasons. The game has taken incredible steps since Naismith's time. Older basketball players are amazed by the agility and blazing speed of modern stars such as Michael Jordan, Charles Barkley, and Shaquille O'Neal.

Basketball is perhaps America's most played sport. Hoops are found on garages in the suburbs and on barn walls in farm areas. To inner-city youth the game of basketball is almost a religion. It is played on inner-city playgrounds during sweltering summer days and on days when ice covers the concrete.

Other popular team sports are hockey, soccer, and volleyball.

Chapter 9

HIGHLIGHTS OF A GREAT NATION

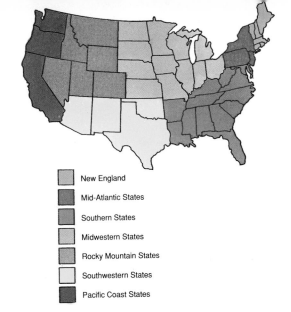

New England

Mid-Atlantic States

Southern States

Midwestern States

Rocky Mountain States

Southwestern States

Pacific Coast States

Geographers often divide the contiguous states into seven major regions: New England, the Mid-Atlantic States, the Southern States, the Midwest, the Mountain States, the Southwest, and the Pacific States. These regions or groups of states have similar landscapes, a common history, and they share the same major industries. The people often speak in a distinctive regional accent. All the major regions offer visitors marvelous outdoor scenery and interesting museums and historic sites.

NEW ENGLAND

The English explorer John Smith sailed along the northeastern coast of the contiguous states in 1614 and named the region New England. The name stuck, especially after Pilgrims, Puritans, and other English colonists settled the land. The New England states are Maine, New Hampshire, Vermont, Massachusetts, Rhode Island, and Connecticut. Proud of their heritage, these states serve as a bedrock of American history.

The awesome cliffs at Maine's Acadia National Park attract more than a million nature-loving tourists a year. Cadillac

Opposite page: Otter Cliffs at Maine's Acadia National Park

Scenes of New England: Boothbay Harbor, Maine (top left); the White Mountains National Forest, New Hampshire (top right); autumn in the town of Brattleboro, Vermont (below left); and Shelburne House in Shelburne, Vermont (below right)

Newbury Street in Boston, Massachusetts

Mountain, which rises in Acadia, is the highest granite mountain on the East Coast. Visitors also flock to Boothbay Harbor, a splendidly restored fishing village nestled near the city of Portland, Maine.

Wilderness wonders adorn New Hampshire and Vermont. New Hampshire's White Mountain National Forest is best seen in the fall, when nature paints the trees with rich colors. Sunapee State Park, near Concord, New Hampshire, is another spot of sweeping natural beauty. The drive between the cities of Bennington and Brattleboro, Vermont, is a breathtaking journey through the Green Mountain National Forest. Vermont history is the theme of the Shelburne Museum near the city of Burlington.

Almost half the population of New England lives in the state of Massachusetts. The state capital, Boston, is one of the nation's most historic cities. Visitors to Boston hike the Freedom Trail,

Mystic Seaport, Connecticut (above) and "The Breakers" built by the wealthy Vanderbilt family in Newport, Rhode Island (right)

which winds past the Boston Massacre site, the birthplace of Benjamin Franklin, and many other monuments of the American past. New Bedford, Massachusetts, was once a major whaling port and is now home to the splendid Whaling Museum. Plymouth Rock, a large boulder at the site where the Pilgrims landed about four hundred years ago, can be seen in the town of Plymouth.

Connecticut and Rhode Island are also bastions of American history. Hartford, Connecticut's capital, boasts the Old State House and the house where Harriet Beecher Stowe lived and wrote *Uncle Tom's Cabin*. Mystic Seaport, on Connecticut's Atlantic shore, is a sprawling museum complex dedicated to New England's seafaring traditions. In the late 1800s fabulously wealthy families built mansions on the rocky seashore near Newport, Rhode Island. These opulent houses can be seen when taking Newport's Cliff Walk. The millionaires who built Newport's mansions used them mainly as summer homes and called them "cottages."

Niagara Falls

THE MID-ATLANTIC STATES

The three mid-atlantic states–New York, New Jersey, and Pennsylvania–prosper by maintaining a healthy blend of agriculture and industry. Visitors to the three states enjoy the sophistication provided by modern cities as well as the natural beauty of these states.

New York is divided into two regions: the New York City area, and the remainder, simply called "upstate." Niagara Falls and the Hudson River valley are scenic highlights of Upstate New York. Interesting side trips along the Hudson include Hyde Park, the birthplace and burial site of Franklin D. Roosevelt, and West Point, the famous United States Military Academy.

New York City is the nation's largest, and in many ways the borough of Manhattan is the nation's most exciting urban center. Central Park, in the center of the city–with a zoo, gardens,

The tall skyscrapers of New York City with the pointed Empire State Building on the right and the Chrysler Building on the extreme left

athletic fields, bike paths, even a lake–provides enjoyment for city dwellers. The city's theaters, restaurants, and music halls are famous throughout the world. Modern art is displayed at New York's Museum of Modern Art and the Guggenheim Museum, medieval paintings hang at the Cloisters, and a wide spectrum of paintings and other art works are shown at the Metropolitan Museum of Art. Massive dinosaur skeletons stand at the city's American Museum of Natural History. Visitors peer into the heavens at New York's Hayden Planetarium. New York City also has architectural marvels such as St. Patrick's Cathedral and the Cathedral of St. John the Divine. At the lower end of Manhattan Island the twin towers of the World Trade Center stand 1,377 feet (420 meters) tall.

New Jersey is a delightful state to visit. Called the Garden State, it has the richest agricultural land in the east. In West

*Central Park (above) and the Metropolitan Museum (right)
in New York City   Below: Fertile Monmouth County
in New Jersey, the Garden State*

*Picturesque hotels (left) are
built along the beach in
Cape May, New Jersey.
Independence Hall (below) in
Philadelphia, Pennsylvania, is a
popular tourist attraction.*

The Liberty Bell

Orange, New Jersey, stands the home and laboratory of Thomas Edison. Replicas of the scientist's major inventions are displayed at the Edison National Historic Site.

The broad state of Pennsylvania spreads westward from the Delaware River. Philadelphia's Independence Hall is where both the Declaration of Independence and the constitution were debated and offered to the people. The Liberty Bell that rang when the Declaration of Independence was adopted in 1776 hangs in Liberty Bell Pavilion. The University of Pittsburgh has a cultural complex that includes a conservatory and a science center. Wellsboro is the gateway to Pennsylvania's "Country Canyon," a sprawling area of forested mountains laced with hiking trails.

THE SOUTHERN STATES

The fourteen southern states spread from the Atlantic seaboard west beyond the Mississippi River. About one-quarter of the country's population lives in the southern states. Mines in West

The frigate Constellation *is moored in the restored Harborplace in Baltimore, Maryland (above); a seventeenth-century house in New Castle, Delaware (top right); the Smithsonian Castle in Washington, D.C. (right)*

Virginia and Kentucky produce much of the nation's coal. Principal crops grown in the southern states include cotton, tobacco, and soybeans. The South is a beautiful land, blessed with a gentle climate and steeped in history.

The nation's oldest warship, the frigate *Constellation,* rests at anchor in a refurbished marina in Baltimore, Maryland. Nearby New Castle, Delaware, was settled in 1651 and contains many restored homes. Washington, D.C., is part of every American's heritage. Touring the museum buildings of the Smithsonian Institution is a high point of any visit to the nation's capital. The Smithsonian displays items ranging from ancient Egyptian relics to rocks taken from the surface of the moon.

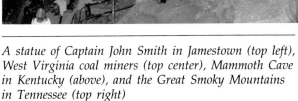

A statue of Captain John Smith in Jamestown (top left),
West Virginia coal miners (top center), Mammoth Cave
in Kentucky (above), and the Great Smoky Mountains
in Tennessee (top right)

English civilization began in the United States with the settlement of Jamestown, Virginia. Statues of Captain John Smith and Pocahontas can be seen at the Jamestown site. Visitors to Beckley, West Virginia, can ride a coal car some 1,000 feet (305 meters) into the side of a mountain. Mammoth Cave in Kentucky is the world's largest cave system. Tourists at Mammoth Cave walk the 12 miles (19 kilometers) of paths past underground rivers, lakes, and waterfalls. The Great Smoky Mountain National Park, which lies mostly in Tennessee, covers 500,000 acres (202,345 hectares). On the park grounds are sixteen major mountain peaks and more than 600 miles (966 kilometers) of clear, rushing streams and rivers.

The lighthouse at Cape Hatteras (left) and an aerial view of Charleston, South Carolina (right)

North Carolina and South Carolina are two of the south's most attractive states. The Cape Hatteras National Seashore in North Carolina consists of 70 miles (113 kilometers) of unspoiled beaches. Also on the North Carolina coast is the historic city of Wilmington, where the World War II battleship *North Carolina* is docked. Tourist boats leaving Charleston, South Carolina, take visitors to Fort Sumter, where the Civil War began.

Florida is the fastest growing state. During the 1980s the population of Florida jumped 33.4 percent, making it the nation's fourth most populous state. Called the "Sunshine State," Florida lures many Americans who enjoy its mild climate. A popular Florida tourist spot is Orlando's Disney World. The Everglades National Park, on Florida's southern tip, is a subtropical wilderness alive with exotic birds and fantastic vegetation.

Georgia, Alabama, and Mississippi are the "deep south" states, enriched by southern traditions. Macon, Georgia, is a lovely town where many pre-Civil War homes are open for public viewing. The Tuskegee Institute in Alabama was established in 1881 to educate the newly freed slaves. Tuskegee's faculty included the famous African-American educators Booker T. Washington and

*Above: Everglades National Park has many
exotic birds, such as the fish-eating anhinga (inset).
Left: A statue of Booker T. Washington stands
at Tuskegee Institute. Below: The Hay House,
a pre-Civil War home in Macon, Georgia*

BOOKER T. WASHINGTON
1856   1915

Vicksburg National Military Park (above right) in Mississippi is the site
of a Civil War battle. Bathhouses line a street in Hot Springs,
Arkansas (above left). The French Quarter (below) in New Orleans
is renowned for good restaurants and good music.

Jazz is performed in Preservation Hall in New Orleans.

George Washington Carver. Vicksburg, Mississippi, was the site of bloody fighting during the Civil War. Today students and tourists walk the battlefields at Vicksburg National Military Park.

West of the Mississippi River sprawl the states of Arkansas and Louisiana. Hot Springs, Arkansas, is a famous health spa where people who hope to increase their blood circulation or ease the pain of arthritis soak in the city's fifteen certified bathhouses. New Orleans is Louisiana's largest city, and a world-renowned entertainment center. The uniquely American musical form–jazz–can be heard on New Orleans streets day and night. New Orleans is also famous for its restaurants.

THE MIDWESTERN STATES

The nation's Midwest is made up of twelve states that spread from the Great Lakes region to the Rocky Mountains. Huge factory centers such as the steel mills of northern Indiana and the

*A covered bridge in Brown County, Indiana (left) and
the Football Hall of Fame in Canton, Ohio (right)*

automobile plants in Michigan give the Midwest industrial
muscle. But the Midwest is also America's "bread basket." Its
farms grow more corn and other grain than any other agricultural
area in the world. One of Indiana's prettiest spots is Brown
County at the southern end of the state. Landscape painters are
drawn to Brown County's rich forests and quaint covered bridges.

The state of Ohio offers visitors a host of cultural attractions.
Masterpieces hang in the Cincinnati Art Museum and wondrous
exhibits thrill guests at the Cincinnati Museum of Natural History.
Football fans flock to Canton, Ohio, home of the Pro Football Hall
of Fame. Residents of Cleveland are proud of the Cleveland
Museum of Art, the Cleveland Aquarium, and the city's
outstanding zoo.

Galena, Illinois, is a handsome river town resplendent with
Victorian houses. To the south is Springfield, Illinois, where
President Abraham Lincoln lived. The Civil War president's house
has been restored and receives hundreds of tourists each day.

Above: A fountain graces the front of the Cleveland Museum of Art. The Belvedere House in Galena, Illinois (below left) and Abraham Lincoln's home in Springfield, Illinois (below right) are two famous historical sites in the Midwest.

Chicago's Grant Park fronts on Lake Michigan (above). The John Hancock Building (right) is the third-tallest building in Chicago. Cold waves of Lake Superior break onto the rocks of Michigan's Upper Peninsula (below).

Living History Farms in Des Moines, Iowa (left), Grand Portage
National Monument in Minnesota (right), and Summerfest
celebration in Milwaukee, Wisconsin (right inset)

Chicago is the Midwest's largest city. Along Chicago's lakefront
are museums, art galleries, shops, and miles of parks.

The Great Lakes give the states of Wisconsin, Michigan, and
Minnesota long and lovely shorelines. Grand Portage National
Monument in Minnesota winds along the shores of Lake Superior.
Hikers and canoeists at Grand Portage experience the rugged
travel conditions faced by early French fur traders. In Dearborn,
Michigan, Greenfield Village holds a collection of ninety-two
historic buildings that were refurbished and moved to the spot by
the pioneer automaker, Henry Ford. Old World Wisconsin presents
a remarkable opportunity to experience the trials and triumphs
faced by the state's pioneers.

Effigy Mountains National Monument in Iowa contains
mysterious structures created by the mound-building people who
lived in the Midwest many centuries ago. In nearby Des Moines,
Iowa, is the Living History Farms, a museum complex dedicated

Main Street in Hannibal, Missouri, the "Show Me" state (above)
A statue honors the buffalo at North Dakota's state capitol (right).

to early Midwestern agriculture. Hannibal, Missouri, is the boyhood home of Mark Twain and the setting for his lovable characters, Tom Sawyer and Huckleberry Finn. Every July a whitewashing party is held at a Hannibal fence to celebrate one of Tom Sawyer's most famous pranks.

Fertile farmland prevails over North Dakota and South Dakota, Nebraska, and Kansas. Relics of North Dakota's pioneers are displayed at Bismarck's Hancock State Historical Site. South Dakota's Badlands National Park contains fossils of animals that lived in the Midwest forty million years ago. Another popular South Dakota tourist attraction rises near Rapid City, where the faces of Presidents Washington, Jefferson, Lincoln, and Theodore Roosevelt are carved on Mount Rushmore. Boys Town, Nebraska, is a world-famous community for homeless boys, founded in 1917 by Father Edward Joseph Flanagan. Dodge City, Kansas, was once the home of Western gunfighters Wyatt Earp and Bat Masterson. Front Street, in Dodge City, is a lively recreation of the town's Wild West past.

Mount Rushmore National Monument (above) was designed by Gutzon Borglum.
A statue of Father Flanagan and some of his "boys" (left) at
Boys Town. Nature designed Badlands National Park (below) in
South Dakota. In Dodge City, Kansas, (below) the "sheriff"
and "gunfighters" put on a show for the tourists.

Glacier National Park in Montana is a haven for wildlife. Bighorn sheep (inset) live there.

THE MOUNTAIN STATES

The mountain states are Colorado, Idaho, Montana, Nevada, Utah, and Wyoming, all of which lie along the rugged spine of the Rocky Mountains. Cattle and sheep ranching are major enterprises in the region. The mountain states are nature's world, where cities are few and open ranges endless.

Glacier National Park sprawls over northern Montana. So rugged is the park site that it can be visited only during the summer months. Glacier National Park has 250 clear mountain lakes and is a haven for rare wildlife, including the Rocky

*Skiing in Sun Valley, Idaho (left) and Old Faithful
erupting in Yellowstone National Park, Wyoming (right)*

Mountain goat and sheep. Craters of the Moon National
Monument in Idaho is a fantastic area of volcano cones, lava
flows, natural bridges, and other exotic rock formations. Skiers
claim that Sun Valley, Idaho, has the world's most perfect snow
for their winter sport.

Yellowstone National Park lies mostly in Wyoming, but its
grounds spread into Idaho and Montana. It is the country's oldest
national park and is famous throughout the world for its geysers
and bubbling hot springs. Visitors to Yellowstone are drawn to
Old Faithful Geyser, which erupts every sixty-five minutes, as if
triggered by a fine watch.

The University of Colorado and the surrounding city of Boulder (above) and the Colorado State Capitol in Denver (inset)

Colorado has the greatest population of all the Mountain States. The city of Denver is proud of its art museum and symphony orchestra. The Golden Dome that tops the Colorado State Capitol is a Denver landmark. Boulder is home to the University of Colorado and is known for its excellent park system.

The Great Salt Lake in northern Utah is actually saltier than the ocean. Because of its salt content, swimmers find they can float on the lake's surface with little effort. Nearby Salt Lake City has many shrines to its Mormon founders. In the city's downtown rises the Mormon Temple with six majestic spires. The 375-voice Mormon Tabernacle Choir has entertained Salt Lake City residents and other music lovers for more than one hundred years. Virginia City, Nevada, has been restored to its 1870s appearance when it was a freewheeling silver mining center.

Virginia City (above), an old silver mining center in Nevada, and the Mormon Tabernacle Church on Temple Square (right) in Salt Lake City, Utah

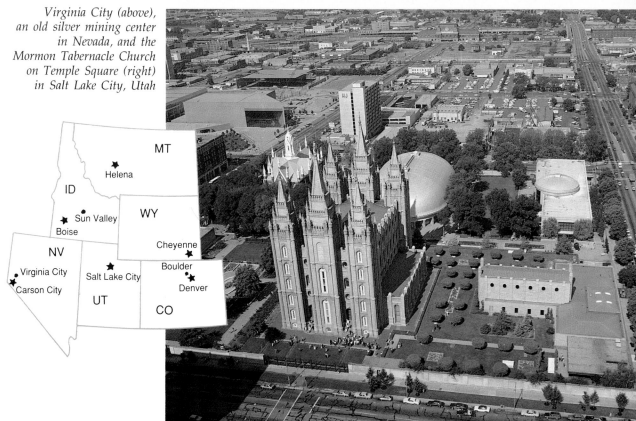

Oklahoma has a working oil well in front of its capitol in Oklahoma City.

THE SOUTHWESTERN STATES

Oklahoma, Texas, New Mexico, and Arizona make up the American Southwest. It is a warm, dry section where farms and cattle ranches prevail. Below the ground is a wealth of oil. Texas and Oklahoma are two of the country's major oil-producing states. The Southwest has been depicted in movies and books as a center of cowboy lore. Guests at Oklahoma's National Cowboy Hall of Fame can relive the storied years when the lonesome cowhand became a national hero.

Texas, which for ten years was an independent nation, has a proud past. A symbol of Texas history is the ancient mission church in San Antonio, the Alamo. In 1836 Texans made a bold stand at the Alamo against an army commanded by Mexico's General Santa Anna. San Antonio also boasts the River Walk, a unique riverbank walkway lined with shops and restaurants.

Above: The Alamo, where Davy Crockett and James Bowie were killed defending Texas. Below: The River Walk in San Antonio

The Grand Canyon

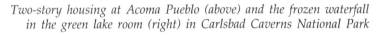

*Two-story housing at Acoma Pueblo (above) and the frozen waterfall
in the green lake room (right) in Carlsbad Caverns National Park*

Along the Rio Grande River spreads Texas's Big Bend National
Park. The park is an amazing field of geological history. Petrified
trees lying on the ground at Big Bend are millions of years old.

Acoma Pueblo, which sits atop a mesa in New Mexico, is the
nation's oldest continually occupied community. More than one
thousand years ago Indians built houses at Acoma, and their
descendants remain there today. Carlsbad Caverns National Park
in southern New Mexico holds the largest underground chamber
known to the world. Tourists at Carlsbad are invited to eat lunch
at a cavern dining room that lies 700 feet (213 meters) below the
ground. Few natural wonders are more thrilling than the Grand
Canyon in northern Arizona. People travel from all over the
world to marvel at the view from the canyon's south rim.

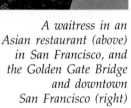

*A waitress in an
Asian restaurant (above)
in San Francisco, and
the Golden Gate Bridge
and downtown
San Francisco (right)*

THE PACIFIC STATES

Stretching along the Pacific shores are the states of California, Oregon, and Washington. An Asian influence is ever present in these states. Asian restaurants and art shops are found in the cities. The landscape of the Pacific states ranges from sunny beaches to snowcapped mountain peaks.

California is the country's most populous state and the leader in agricultural and industrial production. Factories in Los Angeles and San José turn out electrical equipment and military aircraft. The San Francisco Bay area contains the nation's leading

Mt. Lassen in northern California (inset) and vineyards in the Napa-Sonoma area of California

manufacturers of computers and other high-tech items. Farms in California's great Central Valley grow magnificent crops, extending in variety from grapes to cotton.

California is blessed with deep forests, a lovely seacoast, and scenery that embraces deserts as well as mighty forestlands. Death Valley National Monument is a rugged desert landscape where temperatures can soar to 135 degrees Fahrenheit (57.2 degrees Celsius). An eccentric called Death Valley Scotty once built a castle in the midst of this wasteland, and hordes of tourists visit his curious structure today. To the north is California's Lassen Volcanic National Park, the most active volcanic region in the

Yosemite Falls (above) in Yosemite National Park, California, and Crater Lake with Wizard Island in Crater Lake National Park (right), Oregon

United States. Visitors to the park walk carefully over marked trails, while on both sides steam hisses out of rock and lava pools gurgle and bubble. Unparalleled in its beauty is California's Yosemite National Park in the heart of the Sierra Nevada mountain range. Surging waterfalls thrill park guests. The upper and lower Yosemite Falls are among the ten highest waterfalls in North America.

A lighthouse on the rugged Oregon coast

Crater Lake, in Oregon, was formed when water collected in the cone of a vast ancient volcano. Visitors to Crater Lake National Park hike to the cone's peak and gaze down at the lake's blue waters. Lovely and lonely, the Oregon coastline has few houses and no large cities. Instead, the coast is nature's realm, where sea lions bark on surf-washed rocks and waterfowl glide over stark cliffs. More than fifty state parks line Oregon's coast, and the view from the parks belongs to everyone.

The crown of the Pacific states is Washington, whose economy thrives from industry, agriculture, and lumbering. Factories in the Seattle area assemble huge passenger jets for the world's airlines. Orchards in eastern Washington produce the state's juicy apples. Spreading over Washington's Pacific Coast is Olympic National Park, a world of dense forests, diamond-clear lakes, and ferocious rivers. Fir trees in the Olympic Rain Forest grow as high as a fifteen-story office building. Washington's Mount Rainier National Park challenges climbers to scale the mountain's 14,400-foot (4,389-meter) peak. On a clear day, snowcapped Mount Rainier can be seen from downtown Seattle, more than 60 miles (97 kilometers) away.

Above: The skyline of Seattle with Mt. Rainier in the background. Opposite page: Mt. Rainier and Reflection Lake in Mt. Rainier National Park, Washington

Fireweed in bloom in Denali National Park (above), Alaska, and a tour boat on the Columbia Glacier (above left)

AK

Juneau

ALASKA AND HAWAII

Sprawling Alaska is almost one-fifth as large as all the contiguous states combined. Yet for many years Alaska had fewer residents than any other state. It is a land of vast spaces where unspoiled nature prevails. Alaska's Denali National Park is a wildlife haven, home to caribou, mountain sheep, and grizzly bears. Glacier National Park presents the Arctic in all its wonders. Tour boats leave Glacier Bay to take passengers alongside monster icebergs when the giants are breaking up under the summer sun.

Kee Beach (left) on Kauni, Hawaii, and the Arizona Memorial (above), which covers the battleship Arizona

Pristine beaches and warm Pacific waters welcome travelers to Hawaii. Ocean breezes give the island state a pleasant year-round climate. Pearl Harbor, on the island of Oahu, was the site of the 1941 air raid that plunged America into World War II. A monument marks the grave of the battleship U.S.S. *Arizona* that was sunk by a rain of bombs. Sea Life Park, also on Oahu, is a preservation area where visitors enjoy the antics of performing

Akaka Falls, Hawaii

porpoises. Akaka Falls on Hawaii Island is a delicate ribbon of water that tumbles 400 feet (122 meters) into a wooded gorge.

Hawaii is called the Aloha State because visitors are welcomed there with the word *aloha*, meaning "love" in the old Hawaiian language. But even though Hawaii has such a charming greeting, the island state in the Pacific is also a fitting place to end a tour of the United States.

A group of American high school students watching a ball game

THE FUTURE

The United States has become a powerful nation. The men and women of other countries who emigrated here, whether by force or by choice, have given the country its diversity. What will the citizens of this democracy do in the twenty-first century?

More than 150 years ago the poet Henry Wadsworth Longfellow likened America to a ship bearing the world's aspirations when he wrote:

> Thou, too, sail on, O Ship of State!
> Sail on, O Union, strong and great!
> Humanity with all its fears,
> With all the hopes of future years,
> Is hanging breathless on thy fate!

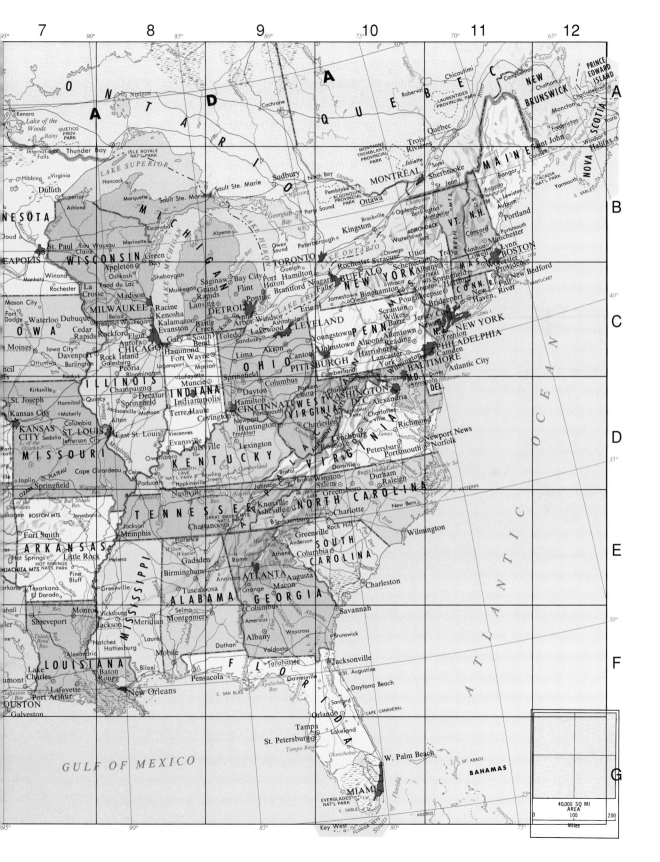

MAP KEY

MINI FACTS AT A GLANCE

GENERAL INFORMATION

Official Name: United States of America

Capital: Washington, D.C.

Government: The United States is a federal republic composed of a national government and 50 state governments. The constitution divides the federal government into three equal branches: executive, legislative, and the judicial. The executive branch is headed by the president who is head of the state and commander-in-chief of the armed forces. Congress is made up of two legislative houses: the Senate with 100 members and the House of Representatives with 435 members. The Supreme Court is the highest judicial body; its nine members are appointed to lifetime terms by the president with the consent of the Senate. Two political parties dominate electoral politics in U. S.: the Democratic party and the Republican party.
There are 50 states and the District of Columbia, or Washington, D.C. American Samoa, Puerto Rico, Guam, the Virgin Islands, and Midway Islands are some of the territories affiliated with the U.S.

Religion: There is no official religion; the U.S. constitution guarantees freedom of religion to all. Some 86 percent of the population is Christian (of which Protestant denominations are 52 percent; Roman Catholic, 34 percent), 4 percent Jewish, 1.8 percent Muslim, and 8.2 percent others. The largest Protestant denominations are the Baptists, Methodists, Lutherans, Pentecostals, and Presbyterians.

Ethnic Composition: Some 80 percent of the total population is of the white race (including Hispanics), 12 percent African-American, 1.5 percent Asian, 0.5 percent American Indians, and the rest from other races. The population is derived primarily from the Anglo-Saxon ethnic group, followed by Hispanic, African, Asian, German, Semitic, Italian, Slavic, Greek, and Celtic. American Indians and Eskimos are the earliest settlers.

Language: English is the official language. A significant minority speaks Spanish.

National Flag: Popularly known as "Old Glory," the U.S. flag is comprised of thirteen alternate stripes, seven red and six white, with fifty, five-pointed white stars (representing the states) placed in nine horizontal rows alternately of six and five against a blue field in the upper left corner. The stripes represent the 13 original colonies.

National Emblem: Adopted in 1782, the emblem has two sides: the face has an eagle with spread wings grasping a green olive branch with 13 leaves and 13 silver arrows in its claws. Its beak holds a scroll with the Latin motto *E Pluribus Unum,* "One Out of Many." The other side has a pyramid with an all-seeing eye of Providence at the summit; at the base the year 1776 is marked in Roman numerals.

National Anthem: "The Star-Spangled Banner," adopted in 1931; words written by Francis Scott Key, music by British composer John Stafford Smith

National Bird: Bald eagle (adopted 1782)

National Flower: Rose (adopted 1986)

National Calendar: Gregorian

Money: A U.S. dollar ($) of 100 cents is the official currency

Membership in International Organizations: Caribbean Community and Common Market (CARICOM); Inter-American Development Bank (IDB); International Atomic Energy Agency (IAEA); International Monetary Fund (IMF); International Whaling Commission (IWC); North Atlantic Treaty Organization (NATO); Organization of American States (OAS); United Nations (UN)

Weights and Measures: The Imperial system is used commonly; the metric system is slowly being introduced.

Population: (1993 estimates) 256,300,000; fourth largest in the world; density is 71 persons per sq. mi. (27 persons per sq km); 74 percent urban, 24 percent rural

Cities:

New York 7,322,564
Los Angeles 3,485,398
Chicago. 2,783,726
Houston 1,630,553
Philadelphia 1,585,577
San Diego 1,110,549
Detroit. 1,027,974
Dallas. 1,006,877
Phoenix. 983,403
San Antonio 935,933
San Jose 782,248
Indianapolis 741,952
Baltimore 736,014
San Francisco 723,959

(Population based on 1990 census.)

GEOGRAPHY

Border: The U.S. shares a 3,987 mi. (6,416 km) border with Canada in the north and a 1,933 mi. (3,111 km) border with Mexico in the south. The Pacific Ocean is on the west and the Atlantic Ocean is on the east. Alaska shares a 8,187 mi. (13,176 km) land border with Canada.

Coastlines: Atlantic Ocean, 2,069 mi. (3,330 km)
Pacific Ocean, 1,293 mi. (2,081 km)
Gulf of Mexico, 1,600 mi. (2,575 km)
Hawaii has a coastline of 750 mi. (1,207 km); Alaska's coastline is 6,640 mi. (10,686 km) long.

Land: The U.S. is the fourth-largest country in the world, after Russia, Canada, and China. The diverse landscape includes arid deserts, rain forests, arctic mountains, and tropical beaches.

The continental U.S. can be divided into five major physiographic regions. The Appalachian Mountains and the Atlantic Coastal Plain are in the east and southeast, the Interior lowlands cover most of the midwestern states, the Rockies and other ranges are in the west, and the Western Intermontane Plateaus are within the western ranges. The Continental Divide, the Atlantic-Pacific watershed, runs along the Rocky Mountains.

Geographically the U.S. can be divided into seven major regions: New England (Maine, New Hampshire, Vermont, Massachusetts, Rhode Island, and Connecticut), the Mid-Atlantic States (New York, New Jersey, and Pennsylvania), the Southern States (West Virginia, Kentucky, Maryland, Delaware, Virginia, Tennessee, North and South Carolinas, Florida, Georgia, Alabama, Mississippi, Arkansas, and Louisiana), the Midwest (Indiana, Michigan, Ohio, Illinois, Wisconsin, Minnesota, Iowa, Missouri, North and South Dakotas, Nebraska, and Kansas), the Mountain States (Colorado, Idaho, Montana, Nevada, Utah, and Wyoming), the Southwest (Oklahoma, Texas, New Mexico, and Arizona), and the Pacific States (California, Oregon, and Washington). Alaska, north of Canada, is almost one-fifth as large as all the contiguous states combined. The Hawaiian Islands are in the mid-Pacific Ocean.

Highest Point: Mt. McKinley, 20,320 ft. (6,194 m)

Lowest Point: Death Valley, 282 ft. (986 m) below sea level

Rivers: The Mississippi is the largest river in North America; other important rivers are Arkansas, Brazos, Colorado, Columbia, Missouri, Ohio, Red, Rio Grande, Snake, and Yukon. Niagara Falls in New York State are one of the most photographed falls in the world. Mammoth Cave in Kentucky is the world's largest cave system.

Lakes: The Great Lakes (Michigan, Superior, Huron, Erie, and Ontario) are the world's largest freshwater reserve. These are accessible to oceangoing vessels from the Atlantic through the St. Lawrence Seaway. Other large lakes include Yellowstone, Great Salt, and Okeechobee.

Forests: About 32 percent of the area is forested with another 23 percent under permanent pastures and meadows. Some 7,000 species and subspecies of vegetation are found in the U.S.; it is the leading producer of wood in the world. Eastern forests contain maple, spruce, beech, birch, hemlock, walnut, gum, and hickory. The central hardwood forests support oak, hickory, ash, maple, and walnut. The southern forests have pine, pecan, gum, birch, and sycamore trees. The richest forests are found in the Pacific northwest (Douglas firs, redwood, and Ponderosa pines). Saguaro (giant cactus), yucca, and candlewood forests are in the southwest. Wildflowers bloom in almost all areas.

National Parks: There are a number of national parks, historic parks, historic sites, monuments, preserves, seashores, lakeshores, recreation areas, and scenic trails. Some major parks are the Acadia National Park in Maine, Great Smoky Mountain National Park in Tennessee (with 16 major mountain peaks), Badlands National Park in South Dakota, Glacier National Park in Montana, Yellowstone National Park (the country's oldest) in Wyoming, Yosemite National Park in California, Crater Lake National Park in Oregon, Mount Rainier National Park in Washington, Denali and Glacier National Parks in Alaska, and Carlsbad Caverns National Park in New Mexico. Lassen Volcanic National Park in northern California is the most active volcanic region in U.S.

Wildlife: Large game animals include white-tailed deer, moose, antelope, wolves, bighorn sheep, cougars, caribou, mountain goats, and black bears. Brown and polar bears are found in Alaska. Furbearing animals include muskrat, red and gray foxes, mink, raccoon, beavers, opossums, hare, and various squirrels. Once abundant, the American buffalo (bison) is now found only on select reserves. Birdlife includes loons, wild ducks, geese, gulls, sandpipers, bald eagles, herons, wrens, owls, hummingbirds, swallows, chickadees, finches, robins, cardinals, meadowlarks, and various blackbirds; wild turkey is a popular game bird. Alligators appear in abundance in the southern waterways; they are protected in Florida's Everglades National Park.

Climate: The climate is generally temperate but varies from tropical (Hawaii and Florida) to subarctic (Alaska). The annual rainfall varies from 2 in. (5 cm) in Death Valley, California, to 480 in. (1,219 cm) in Hawaii. Temperatures can go as high as 135° F (57° C) in Death Valley, and as low as (January average) minus 11° F (minus 24° C) in Fairbanks, Alaska. Great temperature extremes occur in the Midwest–Chicago's average temperature ranges from 27° F (-30 C) in January to 75° F (24° C) in July. The number of frost-free days varies from 240 on the Gulf Coast in the south to 120 on the Canada border in the north. The southern states have a warmer winter than the northern ones. Cities in the Northeast and Midwest are often blanketed by blizzards in winter. Hurricanes are common along the Atlantic Coast and the Gulf of Mexico and tornadoes in the southeastern and central states.

Greatest Distance: North to South: 1,598 mi. (2,572 km)
East to West: 2,807 mi. (4,517 km)
(contiguous United States)

Area: 3,618,770 sq. mi. (9,372,571 sq km) includes 79,481 sq. mi. (205,856 sq km) of inland water area, but excludes the Great Lakes area

ECONOMY AND INDUSTRY

Agriculture: About 21 percent of the total land is under cultivation and some one-tenth of this arable area is irrigated. American farmers are one of the most productive in the world; an average farmer can feed his family and 80 other people. The average farm size is large (440 acres; 178 hectares). Since agriculture is highly mechanized, only 3 percent of the American labor force works on the farms. In California's Central Valley, one of the most productive regions in the country, farmers raise as many as four crops a year. Texas leads in beef production; Nebraska and Iowa are the heart of the wheat growing region.

The U.S. accounts for 25 percent of the world's beef supply and 15 percent of the world's grain supply.

The major crops are corn, soybeans, wheat, sugarcane, sugar beets, sorghum, barley, peanuts, almonds, sunflower seeds, beans, rice, cotton, vegetables, and fruits such as oranges, apples, grapes, peaches, pears, grapefruit, and pineapples. Raw and refined sugar, wine, beer, and honey are produced in large quantities.

Livestock includes cattle, pigs, horses, sheep, goats, and poultry. Dairying is mechanized and well-developed; Wisconsin is called "America's Dairyland" because of its devotion to livestock and milk, cheese, and butter products. Cattle hide and wool production supports leather and textile industries. Cattle and sheep ranching are the major enterprises in the Mountain States.

Fishing: The U.S. ranks among the world's leading fishing nations. Fish catch includes Alaska pollock, menhaden, anchovies, hakes, halibut, mackerel, tuna, whiting, Pacific Salmon, Pacific cod, sea herring, and shellfish such as clams, crabs, lobsters, oysters, scallops, shrimps, and squids.

Mining: About one percent of the U.S. labor force works in mining. Mineral wealth includes petroleum, natural gas, coal, iron ore, phosphate rock, lime, gypsum, aluminum, copper, zinc, lead, magnesium, molybdenum, tin, uranium, silver, and gold. The U.S. is the world's second-largest petroleum and natural gas producer; it also is among the world's leading producers of mica, barite, sulfur, and feldspar. Nuclear energy generates some 20 percent of the total energy used.

Manufacturing: The U.S. has 500,000 major industrial plants and many more light assembly firms. About 20 million people hold manufacturing jobs. Manufacturing began to shift from heavy durable goods to electronics, computers, and software in the 1970s and 80s. The major manufacturing items are steel, automobiles, trucks, buses, airplanes, paper and paperboard, wood pulp, fertilizers, computers, chemicals, synthetic rubber, machine tools, textiles, carpets and rugs, footwear, tires, batteries, household appliances, television sets, radio receivers, and processed foods. California is the leading state in manufactured products; the San Francisco Bay area is the nation's leading manufacturer of computers and other high-tech items. Factories in the Seattle area assemble huge passenger jets for the world's airlines.

Transportation: The national transport network of railways and roads is the largest in the world (in length). The railroad system is 150,000 mi. (241,400 km) long, and the road network is 3,900,000 mi. (6,276,270 km) long, of which some 60 percent of the roads are paved. Modern superhighways crisscross the country. Airports with scheduled flights number about 800, but all together there are 17,000 airports and airfields. Chicago's O'Hare International Airport is the busiest in the world. Great Lakes and inland waterways provide freight facilities. There are some 2,550 mi. (4,104 km) of inland waterways. New York and New Orleans are the biggest among some 50 ports handling ocean cargo traffic. Mass transit includes subways, buses, and local trains in most of the urban areas. New York City, San Francisco, Chicago, Atlanta, Baltimore, Philadelphia, and Washington, D.C. have extensive subway systems. There are 55 automobiles for every 100 people–one of the highest ratios in the world.

Space Research: The American space research program is one of the most sophisticated in the world. *Explorer 1* was the first earth-orbiting satellite launched in 1958. *Vikings 1 and 2* landed equipment on Mars for conducting experiments. In 1977 *Voyager 1 and 2* were launched to travel to Jupiter, Saturn, Uranus, and Neptune. *Columbia* space shuttle, launched in 1981, was the first in a series of reusable manned vehicles. Operational flights were resumed in 1988 after the *Challenger* explosion of 1986. The space shuttle *Discovery* launched an orbiting space telescope in 1990. By 1991 space shuttle vehicles had undertaken a total of 41 operational missions.

Communication: Daily newspapers number about 1,700, with a total circulation of 60,000,000. More than 1,200 weekly and monthly magazines are published. Each year $11 billion worth of books are sold in U.S. In the early 1990s there was one radio receiver per 0.5 persons; one television set per 1.2 persons, and one telephone per 2 persons.

Trade: In 1991 the trade balance was minus 99 billion dollars. The chief imports are machinery and transport equipment (motor vehicles and parts), mineral fuels, and chemicals. The major import sources are Japan, Canada, Mexico, the United Kingdom, Germany, China, South Korea, France, Italy, Saudi Arabia, Hong Kong, and Taiwan. The chief export items are machinery, automobiles, computers, special purpose engines, chemicals, corn, wheat, beef, soybeans, and other agricultural products. The major export destinations are Canada, Japan, Mexico, the United Kingdom, Germany, South Korea, France, the Netherlands, Taiwan, Belgium, Australia, and Singapore.

EVERYDAY LIFE

Health: The United States has one of the best and most technologically advanced health care systems in the world. However, health care is very expensive and out of reach for some Americans. Government-funded programs such as Medicaid (for the poor) and Medicare (for people over age 65) assure medical care for the needy. There is no single national health care system; in 1993 work was in progress to create a system of affordable and less expensive health care for all Americans.

The major illnesses are heart disease, cancers, pneumonia, diabetes, acquired immune deficiency syndrome (AIDS), and cirrhosis. Life expectancy at 70.5 years for males and 77.8 years for females is high. The infant mortality rate at 10.3 per 1,000 is high compared to other industrialized nations. In the early 1990s, there were 391 persons per physician.

Education: Education in most states is free and compulsory between the ages of six and 16 to 18 years. Many children aged 3 and 4 attend nursery schools, and some 95 percent of children aged 5 attend kindergarten. About 80 percent of the elementary and secondary schools in U.S. are public where education is free. Although education is state supported, school lunch programs are supported by the federal government. Many private schools are run by religious institutions. There are more than 3,500 two-year and four-year colleges and universities. The U.S. has some of the finest institutions of higher education in the world such as Harvard University in Boston; Yale University in New Haven, Massachusetts; Princeton University in Princeton, New Jersey; the University of Chicago in Chicago; and the University of Texas in Austin. In the early 1990s the literacy rate was about 96 percent.

Holidays:

New Year's Day, January 1
Martin Luther King, Jr. Day, third Monday in January
President's Day, third Monday in February
Memorial Day, last Monday in May
Independence Day, July 4
Labor Day, first Monday in September
Columbus Day, second Monday in October
Veteran's Day, November 11
Thanksgiving Day, fourth Thursday in November
Christmas, December 25

Culture: Many outstanding authors, composers, and artists are products of American culture. Several distinctive types of popular music have been developed in the U.S., such as jazz, the blues, country and western, and rock and roll. Blues are the mournful songs that African slaves used to sing while working in the fields. Jazz is a uniquely American form of music, originated from a blend of ragtime music and blues. American motion pictures have been one of the most popular and internationally influential art forms. Hollywood, California, is generally considered the motion picture capital of the world.

There are some 7,000 museum in the U.S. Art is displayed at the Museum of Modern Art, Guggenheim Museum, and Metropolitan Museum of Art in New York and at other art museums throughout the country. Other well-known museums are the American Museum of Natural History in New York, Smithsonian Institution in Washington, D.C., and Field Museum of Natural History and Museum of Science and Industry in Chicago.

The U.S. has about 8,000 public and 5,000 private libraries, and many school and college libraries. Notable among government buildings are the White House (President's residence), the Capitol building, and the Supreme Court building in Washington, D.C.

Society: Economically the U.S. is one of the world's most developed countries. Americans enjoy one of the world's highest standards of living. Most Americans are from the working middle class. They are teachers, nurses, firefighters, storekeepers, and electricians. A small percentage of people are very wealthy. A large percentage lives in suburbs of big cities, and own two or three automobiles. American women were given the right to vote in 1920 by the Nineteenth Amendment. American women joined the work force in large numbers during World War II. The National Organization for Women (NOW) has crusaded for equality of opportunities for women, especially in the workplace.

Housing: Almost all houses have electricity and clean running water in urban areas. Families enjoy video recorders, televisions, stereos, dishwashers, clothes washers and dryers, and vacuum cleaners. Most rural Americans live in single-family houses with a number of modern amenities. In big cities like New York, Chicago, Los Angeles, and Detroit, large public-housing projects are the less-than-satisfactory home of many poor inner-city people.

Food: The American diet is perhaps the most varied in the world. People in general have access to meat and dairy products, fruits, and vegetables. Breakfast can vary from a bowl of cereal with milk and fruit to pancakes with bacon or sausages. Americans drink a lot of coffee and cola, and smaller amounts of tea, milk, wine, and juices. A typical meal may include meat, potatoes, lettuce salad, some vegetable, and bread. Hamburgers and hot dogs are the most popular American lunch items. Cakes, cookies, ice cream, and pies are eaten as snacks and desserts. Fast-food restaurants are almost an essential part of urban areas.

Sports and Recreation: Americans enjoy sports. American athletes enjoy immense popularity. Baseball is called the national pastime; it is played in city school yards and in rural sand lots. American football has evolved from soccer, and is one of the most watched TV programs during the football season. The whole nation comes to a halt during the Super Bowl game. Basketball was invented in Springfield, Massachusetts, in 1891; it is America's most played sport. Other popular team sports are hockey, soccer, and volleyball. Favorite recreational activities are watching spectator sports, home gardening, jogging, swimming, aerobic exercise, tennis, golfing, skiing, sailing, boating, rafting, and canoeing.

Most Americans travel in their leisure time. Traveling in motor homes or trailers is very popular. Disney World in Florida is one of the most popular tourist spots. New Orleans, Atlantic City, and Las Vegas are world-renowned entertainment centers. Mount Rushmore in South Dakota with carved faces of presidents Washington, Jefferson, Lincoln, and Theodore Roosevelt is another popular tourist attraction.

Social Welfare: State and federally funded programs provide financial help to people without jobs; they include Supplemental Security Income (SSI) and Aid to Families with Dependent Children (ADC). Social benefits cover unemployment, work injury, sickness, maternity, old age, and disability. After retirement Americans receive monthly Social Security payments from the Federal Social Security Fund. Several religious groups provide aid for refugees, the poor and homeless, the elderly, orphans, and other persons in need.

IMPORTANT DATES

1492–Christopher Columbus "discovers" America

1565–Spaniards establish the city of St. Augustine, the oldest permanent settlement in the U.S., on the eastern coast of Florida

1585–The British settle a colony on Roanoke Island, off the coast of North Carolina

1607–English colonists establish the first permanent colony of Jamestown in Virginia

1610–Spaniards establish city of Santa Fé

1620–The Pilgrims from *Mayflower* establish Plymouth Colony in Massachusetts

1632–English Roman Catholics build colonies on the Maryland shore

1692–Nineteen residents believed to be witches are hanged in Salem, Massachusetts

1756-1763–French and Indian War

1770–British soldiers are jeered in Boston; soldiers kill five people in the "Boston Massacre"

1775–Gun fighting erupts between British soldiers and colonists in Concord, Massachusetts; George Washington leads an army to fight the British soldiers

1776–The Declaration of Independence is issued

1777–Colonists defeat a British invasion from Canada at the Battle of Saratoga

1778–France declares war on England

1781–American-French army defeats the British at Yorktown, Virginia

1787–The U.S. constitution is written during the Constitutional Convention in Philadelphia; the Northwest Ordinance is passed by Congress

1790–The first census is taken; 95 percent of the U.S. population lives in rural areas

1791–The Bill of Rights, the ten original amendments to the U.S. constitution, is passed

1803–The Louisiana Purchase adds almost 900,000 sq. mi. (2,331,000 sq km) to the United States

1836–American settlers in Texas break away from Mexico and form a separate republic

1846–The Mexican War; Great Britain drops its claims on Washington and Oregon territories

1848–Gold is discovered in California

1849–Some 85,000 gold seekers swarm to California

1860–Abraham Lincoln is elected president; seven southern states secede from the Union to form the Confederate States of America

1861–Confederate artillery fires on Federal troops at Fort Sumter; American Civil War begins (ends 1865)

1863–Battle of Gettysburg; Union forces defeat Confederate armies; President Lincoln issues the Emancipation Proclamation freeing all slaves; African-Americans are recruited in the Union army

1865–Confederate General Lee surrenders to Union General Grant; Civil War ends; the Thirteenth Amendment to the constitution ends slavery

1867–The U.S. purchases Alaska from Russia for $7,200,000

1868–The Fourteenth Amendment gives African-Americans the right to vote

1869–The transcontinental railroad opens

1871–A great fire destroys Chicago's business district

1877–Reconstruction ends as federal troops are withdrawn from the former Confederate states

1889–Thomas Edison invents moving pictures

1892–The federal government builds an immigration processing center at Ellis Island

1898–The U.S. takes possession of the Hawaiian Islands; the Spanish-American War; U.S. acquires Guam, the Philippines, and Puerto Rico

1903–The U.S. purchases a narrow strip of land across the Isthmus of Panama to build the Panama Canal

1917–The U.S. enters World War I (began in 1914 and ended in 1918)

1919–The Eighteenth Amendment to the constitution prohibits the sale of alcohol

1920–The census marks, for the first time, that more people live in cities than in rural areas

1924–A law passed by Congress makes all native Indians citizens of the U.S.

1927–Charles Lindbergh makes a solo flight across the Atlantic Ocean

1929–The New York Stock Exchange crashes as part of the Great Depression

1932–Franklin Delano Roosevelt is elected president

1935–The Social Security Act is passed

1941–Japan attacks U.S. base on Pearl Harbor; the U.S. enters World War II (ends 1945)

1942–American naval forces defeat Japanese fleet near Midway Island

1944–American forces participate in D-Day invasion of France; Phillipine Islands are retaken by American naval and land forces

1945–The U.S. drops atomic bombs on Hiroshima and Nagasaki in Japan; World War II ends

1946–The Philippines are granted independence

1950–The U.S. intervenes to stop North Korean invasion of South Korea

1952–Dwight D. Eisenhower is elected president

1953–Korean War ends

1954–The U.S. Supreme Court outlaws segregation in public schools; the U.S. explodes the first hydrogen bomb

1955–Civil Rights Movement begins in Alabama

1960–John F. Kennedy is elected president; the Civil Rights Act gives voting rights to all Americans

1961–President Kennedy launches Bay of Pigs invasion of Communist Cuba; the Peace Corps is launched

1962–U.S. blockades Cuba; Soviets withdraw their missiles from Cuba; U.S. sends astronaut John Glenn into space orbit

1963–President Kennedy is assassinated; Atomic Test-Ban Treaty is signed; Martin Luther King, Jr., leads 200,000 African-Americans and whites in the Civil Rights March in Washington, D.C.

1964–Congress passes the Civil Rights Act, ending segregation in all businesses open to the public

1965–The U.S. begins bombing of North Vietnam and sends combat forces to South Vietnam, adding to the 17,000 advisors already there

1968–Martin Luther King, Jr., and Robert F. Kennedy are assassinated in separate incidents; Nuclear Nonproliferation Treaty is signed; about half a million U.S. troops are involved in the Vietnam War; Richard Nixon is elected president

1969–U.S. astronaut Neil A. Armstrong lands on the moon

1970–National Guard soldiers kill four protesting students at Kent State University, Ohio

1972–Nixon is reelected as president; Nixon visits Peking; beginning of Watergate Scandal

1973–Vietnamese peace agreement is signed; Congress passes the War Powers Resolution over President Nixon's veto

1974–The Watergate affair becomes a major national crisis; Nixon resigns; Gerald Ford becomes president

1975–North Vietnam forces unification of the country

1976–Jimmy (James E.) Carter is elected president

1977–The U.S. and Panama sign the Panama Canal treaties

1979–The U.S. officially recognizes the People's Republic of China and breaks off diplomatic relations with Taiwan, but continues social and economic ties; the U.S. embassy is seized in Teheran, Iran

1980–The U.S. boycotts Summer Olympics in Moscow; Ronald Reagan is elected president; census counts over 160 cities with a population of more than 100,000; Mt. St. Helens erupts in Washington state

1981–U.S. hostages are freed in Teheran

1984–Reagan is reelected as president

1986–Space shuttle *Challenger* explodes shortly after liftoff

1987–The stock market collapses

1988–George Bush is elected president

1990–The U.S. is involved in the Persian Gulf War against Iraq

1992–Hurricane Andrew kills 52 people and leaves a quarter of a million people homeless in South Florida

1993–The Midwest suffers one of the worst Mississippi river floods

IMPORTANT PEOPLE

Henry Aaron, (1934-), athlete; set new batting records when he played professional baseball; his home run record is 755

Grover Cleveland Alexander (1887-1950, athlete; considered one of the greatest right-hand major league pitchers in baseball

Louis Armstrong (1900-71), called Satchmo; African-American jazz musician; trumpeter; invented scat singing style

Neil Armstrong (1930-), first man to set foot on moon

Crispus Attucks (1723-70), patriot; runaway slave, killed in Boston Massacre

Benjamin Banneker (1731-1806), mathemetician and astronomer; helped survey District of Columbia area

George Bellows (1882-1921), artist and lithographer; known for his landscapes and sports scenes

Thomas Hart Benton (1889-1975), painter; painted realistic people in everyday life

Leonard Bernstein (1918-90), composer, conductor, and teacher of classical music

Daniel Boone (1734-1820), pioneer; guided settlers through Cumberland Gap to the Kentucky region

John Wilkes Booth (1838-65), Shakespearean actor; assassinated President Abraham Lincoln at Ford's Theater, Washington, D.C., April 14, 1865

Daniel Burnham (1846-1912), architect; head of construction for buildings at the 1893 Chicago World's Fair; built the Montauk Building

George Herbert Walker Bush (1924-   ), 41st president

John Cabot (1450-99), Italian navigator and explorer

Stephen Cabot (1476-1557), son of John Cabot; navigator and explorer

Leonard Calvert (1606-47), British colonist Catholic leader

Andrew Carnegie (1835-1919), Scottish immigrant; built a large steel manufacturing empire

James Earl "Jimmy" Carter (1924-   ), 39th president

George Washington Carver (1864-1943), African-American educator; known for his work on industrial application for peanuts

Mary Cassatt (1844-1926), painter; famous for paintings of women and children

Willa Cather (1873-1947), novelist; works include *O Pioneers*, *My Antonia*, and *Death Comes for the Archbishop*

George Catlin (1796-1872), author and wilderness painter; painted Indians and Indian life; wrote about Indian life

Samuel de Champlain (c.1567-1635), French explorer; explored the St. Lawrence River area and organized the fur trade in northeastern North America

William Clark (1770-1838), soldier and explorer; with Meriwether Lewis, explored the wilderness territory of Louisiana Purchase

William Jefferson Clinton (1946-   ), 42nd president; governor of Arkansas from 1978 to 1980, and again from 1982 to 1992

Ty Cobb (1886-1961), called the "Georgia Peach"; athlete; known for his hitting and offensive playing; received the most votes on the first balloting for the Baseball Hall of Fame in 1936

George M. Cohan (1878-1942), actor, playwright, and producer; associated with Broadway plays; wrote song "Over There," which was popular during World War I

Christopher Columbus (1451-1506), Italian explorer; "discovered" the New World of America in 1492

Thomas Cole (1801-48), landscape painter; founder (with Asher Durand) of the Hudson River School of landscape

James Fenimore Cooper (1789-1851), novelist; remembered for works such as *The Spy*, *The Last of the Mohicans*, and *The Pathfinder*

Aaron Copland (1900-90), composer; works include ballet scores *Billy the Kid*, *El Salón México*, and *Rodeo*; also remembered for *Appalachian Spring* and other compositions

John Singleton Copley (1738-1815), painter; did portraits of important political figures of his day

Francisco Vazquez de Coronado (1510-54), Spanish gold seeker; led an army into southwestern U.S. in 1540

Frederick Douglass (1817-95), an escaped slave; author, editor, abolitionist

Asher Durand (1796-1886), engraver and painter; founder (with Thomas Cole) of Hudson River School of landscape

Wyatt Earp (1848-1929), lawman, gambler; subject of legends; deputy marshal in Tombstone, Arizona, during the "Gunfight at O.K. Corral"

Thomas Alva Edison (1847-1931), inventor; best known for lightbulb, phonograph, and talking motion pictures

Jonathan Edwards (1703-58), Puritan clergyman and theologian

Eisenhower, Dwight D. (1890-1969), 34th president; general during World War II

Andrew Ellicott (1754-1820), surveyor

Ralph Ellison (1914-   ), teacher and writer; wrote *Invisible Man*

Ralph Waldo Emerson (1803-82), poet and essayist; remembered for two volumes of *Essays*

Leif Eriksson (eleventh century), explorer; son of Erik the Red; founded land west of Greenland and called it Vinland

William Faulkner (1897-1962) writer; won Nobel Prize for literature in 1949; best known for *The Sound and the Fury*

F. Scott Fitzgerald (1896-1940), writer; chronicled the Jazz Age; works include *The Great Gatsby* and *This Side of Paradise*

Father Edward Joseph Flanagan (1886-1948), clergyman; founded Boys Town for orphaned boys

Henry Ford (1863-1947), automobile manufacturer; used an assembly line to produce the Model T Ford

Gerald Ford (1913-   ), 38th president

Stephen Collins Foster (1826-64), American songwriter; songs include "Oh! Susanna" and "My Old Kentucky Home"

Benjamin Franklin (1706-90), writer, inventor, businessman, diplomat, and statesman

George Gershwin (1898-1937), composer of classical and popular music

John Glenn (1921-   ), the first U.S. astronaut to orbit the earth; became U.S. senator from Ohio

Ulysses Simpson Grant (1822-85), Union general; 18th president

D.W. Griffith (1875-1948), motion picture director

Marvin Hamlisch (1944-   ), composer; musicals include *A Chorus Line*, the longest running show on Broadway (1975 to 1990)

Oscar Hammerstein (1895-1960), lyricist; considered one of the greatest lyricists in the American musical theater; wrote lyrics for successful musicals including *Oklahoma, The Sound of Music,* and *South Pacific*

Bret Harte (1863-1902), writer; wrote about mining in the west in *The Luck of Roaring Camp and Other Sketches*; was U.S. consul in Prussia and Scotland

Ernest Hemingway (1899-1961), writer; best known for *A Farewell to Arms* and *For Whom the Bell Tolls*; won Nobel Prize for literature in 1954

Woody Herman (1913-87), jazz musician, vocalist, and bandleader; his band was called the Thundering Herd

Edward Hopper (1882-1967), painter; known for realistic scenes of everyday life

John Huston (1906-87), movie director; known for *Treasure of the Sierra Madre* (1944)

Washington Irving (1783-1859), writer; famous for short stories including "Rip Van Winkle"

Thomas Jefferson (1743-1826), architect; 3rd president; chief writer of the Declaration of Independence; founder of the U.S. political party system

William Le Baron Jenney (1832-1907), architect; used steel skeleton construction, which made the building of skyscrapers possible

Andrew Johnson (1808-75), 17th president; vice-president under Lincoln

Lyndon Baines Johnson (1908-73), 36th president

John H. Johnson (1918-   ), publisher, first published *Ebony* in 1945

Scott Joplin (1868-1917), composer; known for composing ragtime music such as "Maple Leaf Rag" and "The Entertainer"

John Fitzgerald Kennedy (1917-63), 35th president; established the Peace Corps

Reverend Martin Luther King, Jr., (1929-68), civil rights leader; won the Nobel Peace Prize in 1964

Pierre Charles L'Enfant (1754-1825), architect and soldier; planned Washington, D.C. as the nation's capital

Robert Cavelier, Sieur de La Salle (1643-87), French explorer and fur trader

Robert Edward Lee (1807-70), Confederate general from Virginia

Alan Jay Lerner (1918-86), lyricist; collaborated with Frederick Loewe; wrote such Broadway musicals as *Brigadoon* and *Camelot*

Meriwether Lewis (1774-1809), explored with William Clark the wilderness territory of the Louisiana Purchase

Abraham Lincoln (1809-65), lawyer; 16th president; led country through the Civil War

Charles Lindbergh (1902-74), pioneer aviator; made the first solo flight across the Atlantic Ocean in 1927

Frederick Loewe (1904-88), composer; collaborated with Alan Jay Lerner; remembered for *My Fair Lady* and many other musicals

Henry Wadsworth Longfellow (1807-82), poet; works include "The Village Blacksmith" and "Paul Revere's Ride"

Joe Louis (1914-81), called "The Brown Bomber"; boxer; successfully defended his world heavyweight title 25 times

James Madison (1751-1836), scholar and lawyer from Virginia; 4th president

Malcolm X (1925-65), originally named Malcolm Little; religious leader; converted to Black Muslim faith and changed his name while in prison for robbery; preached black pride; broke with Black Muslims to form his own religious group

George Mason (1725-92), statesman; member of Continental Congress; refused to sign the U.S. constitution because of his opposition to slavery

William Barclay Masterson (1853-1921), known as "Bat"; peace officer; associated with Wyatt Earp in Tombstone, Arizona; defended order on the American frontier

Herman Melville (1819-91), writer; best-known book is the classic *Moby Dick*

H.L. Mencken (1880-1956), journalist and writer

Arthur Miller (1915-), playwright; known especially for *Death of a Salesman*

Glenn Miller (1904-44), "big band" bandleader; disappeared in flight from England to France during World War II

Ferdinand Joseph Morton (1885-1941), called "Jelly Roll," musician and composer

Gerry Mulligan (1927-), saxophonist, arranger, and composer; popularized "cool" jazz

James Naismith (1861-1939), physical educator; originated game of basketball

Richard Milhous Nixon (1913-), 37th president; opened diplomatic relations with China; resigned from presidency in 1974

Georgia O'Keeffe (1887-1986), modern artist, famous for her impressions of the Southwest

Eugene O'Neill (1888-1953), playwright; won the Nobel Prize for literature in 1936

Elisha Graves Otis (1811-61), inventor; developed the elevator

Thomas Paine (1737-1809), political philosopher and author; wrote *Common Sense* and *The Rights of Man*

Rosa Parks (1913-), her refusal to yield her bus seat to a white person started the Civil Rights Movement

Mary Pickford (1893-1979), actress

Pocahontas (1595-1617), American Indian princess; helped the starving Jamestown colony people with food

Edgar Allan Poe (1809-49), writer of poems and short stories, considered to be the inventor of the detective story

Jackson Pollock (1912-56), painter; known for dripping or pouring paint onto his canvas

Edwin S. Porter (1870-1941), film director and photographer; worked with Edison as cameraman

Elvis Presley (1935-77), king of rock and roll music

John Rankin, slave sympathizer; part of the "Underground Railroad" helping black slaves to flee north

Paul Revere (1735-1818), silversmith, engraver, and patriot

Jackie Robinson (1919-72), athlete; first black baseball player in major leagues

John Davison Rockefeller (1839-1937), established Standard Oil Company; built a petroleum empire

Richard Rodgers (1902-79), composer; wrote musical comedies, including *Oklahoma, South Pacific,* and *The King and I*

Franklin Delano Roosevelt (1882-1945), 32nd president; elected president four times; led the country during the Great Depression and World War II

Theodore Roosevelt (1858-1919), 26th president (1901 to 1909); added 150 million acres (60,703,500 hectares) to the national forest system; received Nobel Peace Prize in 1906

George Herman "Babe" Ruth (1895-1948), baseball player remembered for hitting home runs

William Seward (1801-72), politician; secretary of state who purchased Alaska from Russia

Upton Sinclair (1878-1968), writer and social reformer; wrote *The Jungle*, which exposed horrible working conditions in the stock yards in Chicago in the early 1900s

Captain John Smith (c.1580-1631), colonist; helped found settlement of Jamestown

John Philip Sousa (1854-1932), bandmaster and composer; called the "The March King"; remembered for marches such as "Stars and Stripes Forever"

Steven Spielberg (1947-), movie director known for his imagination and special effects

Squanto (?-1622), Pawtuxet Indian; taught the Plymouth colonists how to plant and fertilize corn

Harriet Beecher Stowe (1811-96), writer; best known for *Uncle Tom's Cabin*

Louis Henry Sullivan (1856-1924), architect from Chicago School

Harry S Truman (1884-1972), 33rd president

Harriet Tubman (1823-1913), important conductor in the Underground Railroad; helped more than 300 slaves to freedom

Mark Twain (1835-1910), born Samuel Langhorne Clemens; humorist and writer

Rudolph Valentino (1895-1926), actor; matinee idol in silent films

Ludwig Mies van der Rohe (1886-1969), architect; well known for gleaming glass and steel towers of the International Style

Booker Taliaferro Washington (1856-1915), African-American educator; founder of Tuskegee Institute

George Washington (1732-99), leader of the Colonial army; 1st president

Orson Welles (1915-85), motion picture actor, director, producer, and writer; remembered for film *Citizen Kane*

Walt Whitman (1819-92), poet; known for *Leaves of Grass*

Grant Wood (1891-1942), regionalist painter; most famous painting is *American Gothic* of an Iowa farm couple

Frank Lloyd Wright (1867-1959), modern architect; established the Prairie Style

INDEX

Page numbers that appear in boldface type indicate illustrations

About the Author

R. Conrad Stein was born in Chicago. After serving with the marine corps he attended the University of Illinois and was graduated with a degree in history. Mr. Stein is the author of many books and short stories written for young readers. He lives in Chicago with his wife and his daughter Jana.